Robert Ellis Thompson

The National Hymn-Book of the American Churches

Robert Ellis Thompson

The National Hymn-Book of the American Churches

ISBN/EAN: 9783337296681

Printed in Europe, USA, Canada, Australia, Japan

Cover: Foto ©Lupo / pixelio.de

More available books at **www.hansebooks.com**

THE NATIONAL HYMN-BOOK

OF THE

AMERICAN CHURCHES:

COMPRISING

THE HYMNS WHICH ARE COMMON TO THE HYMNARIES

OF THE

Baptists, Lutherans,
Congregationalists, Methodists,
Episcopalians, Presbyterians,
and Reformed,

WITH THE MOST USUAL TUNES.

EDITED BY

ROBERT ELLIS THOMPSON, S.T.D.

PHILADELPHIA:
JOHN D. WATTLES.
1893.

EDITOR'S PREFACE.

This book is not a selection, but a collection. In compiling it the editor has not been guided by his own tastes and preferences. He simply has acted as a "returning judge," certifying which hymns have received the votes of the seven chief churches of American Protestantism. The hymns thus sanctioned constitute a collection, which embraces the best in general use. At the same time they show a remarkable degree of unity in the spirit among the chief branches of our divided Christendom. Rev. James King in his *Anglican Hymnology* (London, 1885) shows that not a single hymn is to be found in all the hymnaries in use in the Church of England. The number common to our church hymnaries of the leading denominations of America is found to be about the same as that of the Hebrew Psalms.

The various sources of these hymns are as noteworthy as is the sanction they have received. The great Anglican communion of both sides the Atlantic holds a decided preponderance among the authors. Next come the Congregationalists or Independents, the Methodists, the Presbyterians, the Baptists, the Moravians, the Roman Catholics and the Unitarians, in about this order.

The arrangement of the book being mainly chronological, it furnishes a means of tracing the development of English hymnody from the close of the seventeenth century to our own times. In Baxter and Ken we have the unpolished style of the older religious poetry. In Watts, Addison, Stennett, Doddridge, Steele and Barbauld, we see how hymn-writing was affected by the literary traditions of the school of Pope, with its "poetical diction," artificial graces, and somewhat monotonous forms of verse. But in the hymns of the Wesleys and their associates in the Methodist movement we find the new wine bursting these old bottles, and religious inspiration taking shapes in more harmony with its own character. In Newton and Cowper we have the blending of both influences.

The present century opens with the effort to introduce high poetry into hymn-writing, made by Grant, Heber, and Milman. But Montgomery and Lyte stand apart from the main current nearly as much as does Campbell in secular poetry. With Keble, hymnody receives its first impact from the great Oxford movement, which was to modify the forms of Christian worship in all denominations, and to enrich our hymnody by treasures drawn from ancient sources. Thanks to that movement a wider interest in hymnology has been diffused, and a large body of writers has been enlisted in hymn-writing, throughout the English-speaking world, so that the last sixty years may fairly be called the golden age of English hymn-writing.

As regards the method on which this book has been compiled, some explanation is needed. It includes no hymn which has not had the sanction of at least one hymn-book of each of the seven denominations mentioned on the title-page. In some cases there was difficulty in ascertaining exactly what books possessed a representative denominational character. In the case of the Baptists, happily, there are three whose claim hardly can be disputed. In that of the Congregationalists, the two Andover hymn-books and the Connecticut Association's collection seem to have an equally good standing. That of Dr. Richards was added as being widely used by the churches of that order, and prepared by one of their pastors. Besides the hymn-books of the Methodist Episcopal Churches, North and South, those of the United Brethren and the Evangelical Association—Methodist bodies of German-American origin—have been added, but no hymn has been counted as having the Methodist vote which was not found in one of the two first named. The Moravian hymn-book has been put in the list because, although the body is a small one, it holds a peculiar place in both the hymnody and the esteem of American Christians. The best known hymn-book of the Disciples is included; but the differences between that body and Evangelical Protestants generally give it a border position, which made it unsuitable to exclude hymns it did not contain. The Reformed Episcopalians also are represented, but hymns have not been excluded because omitted from their book.

Besides the twenty-one denominational hymn-books thus consulted and indexed, there are nine privately edited books to which references are given. It might have been possible to extend this list greatly, but only those have been taken which are in line with the general composition of the hymn-books sanctioned by the churches, and which are in extensive use.

It will be observed that on the right-hand margin of each hymn these thirty hymn-books are so indicated that the hymn in question may be found promptly in any of them that contain it. This makes easy the use of the book in connection with any or several of these, thus fitting it for use in union services, hotel parlors and the like. Besides this, clergymen who are invited to conduct services in a church of another denomination than their own, often have not the means of ascertaining which of the standard hymns they may expect to find in its hymnal. With this book in hand, a selection can be made promptly and accurately.

The book will be found especially suited to educational institutions, which aim at exerting a religious influence in harmony with the common Christianity of our Protestant Churches, to the exclusion of the denominational peculiarities of any of them.

The list of hymns would have been longer but for two circumstances. The first was the requirement that every hymn taken should be found in the hymnal of the Protestant Episcopal Church. The second was the narrowing of even this range by the character of the Lutheran hymnals. In these churches naturally there is a preference for translations of those German hymns which constitute so precious a treasure of the Evangelical Church. The Missouri Synodical Conference has a hymn-book composed entirely of original translations of German hymns; and the admirable hymn-book recently adopted by the Ohio Synod is so rich in such as to have but little room for even the standard English hymns. The same is true to some extent of the Church Book of the Lutheran General Council, and also of the Moravian hymn-book.

In determining the texts, due regard has been had to general American usage; and where there has been no uniformity in variation, preference has been given commonly to the original text.

In the selection of the tunes, general or even partial agreement has been made determinative where this existed. In other cases, the choice has been made of that tune which seemed by its own merits and the adaptation of its melody to the words, to have the best claim. In this part of the work the Editor has been indebted to his friend, Mr. Edwin F. Schively, of Germantown, for valuable suggestions.

LIST OF HYMN-BOOKS USED.

1. [BpC] The Service of Song for Baptist Churches. Enlarged edition. Edited by S. L. Caldwell and A. J. Gordon. Boston. 1875. [1129 hymns.]

2. [BpN] The Baptist Hymnal for Use in Church and Home. Edited by W. Howard Doane and E. H. Johnson. Philadelphia: American Baptist Publication Society. 1883. [704 hymns.]

3. [BpS] The Baptist Praise Book: For Congregational Singing. Prepared by Richard Fuller, etc. J. P. Holbrook, musical editor. New York, Baltimore, etc. 1871. [1311 hymns.]

4. [CoA] Hymns of the Faith, with Psalms, for the Use of Congregations. Edited by George Harris and William Jewett Tucker, professors in Andover Theological Seminary, and Edward K. Glezen. Boston and New York. 1887. [629 hymns.]

5. [CoC] The Book of Praise, or Hymns and Tunes for Public and Social Worship. Prepared [for] the General Association of Connecticut. Hartford. 1868. [974 hymns.]

6. [CoR] Songs of Christian Praise with Music: A Manual of Worship for Public, Social and Private Devotion. Selected and arranged by Charles H. Richards. New York. 1880. [660 hymns.]

7. [CoS] The Sabbath Hymn and Tune Book. Edited by Edwards A. Parks, Austin Phelps and Lowell Mason. Boston. 1858. [1290 hymns.]

8. [Dis] The Christian Hymnal: Revised. A Collection of Hymns and Tunes for Congregational and Social Worship. Cincinnati. 1882. [747 hymns.]

9. [Ep] The Church Hymnal of the Protestant Episcopal Church. 1874. [563 hymns.]

10. [EAs] The Evangelical [Association's] Hymn and Tune Book. Cleveland, Ohio. 1882. [875 hymns.]

11. [LuC] Church Book, for the Use of Evangelical Lutheran Congregations. By authority of the General Council of the Evangelical Lutheran Church in America. Philadelphia. 1868. [588 hymns.]

12. [LuS] Book of Worship with Tunes. Published by the General Synod of the Lutheran Church in the United States. Philadelphia. 1880. [601 hymns.]

13. [MEN] Hymnal of the Methodist Episcopal Church. New York. 1878. [1117 hymns.]

14. [MES] A Collection of Hymns and Tunes for Public, Social and Domestic Worship. Nashville: Southern Methodist Publishing Co. 1874. [842 hymns.]

15. [Mor] Offices of Worship and Hymns (with Tunes) Published by Authority

of the American Province of the Unitas Fratrum or the Moravian Church. Third edition. Revised and enlarged. Bethlehem. 1891. [1516 hymns.]

    16. [PrN] The Presbyterian Hymnal. Philadelphia. 1874. [972 hymns.]

    17. [PrS] Book of Hymns and Tunes. Richmond: Presbyterian Committee of Publication. [852 hymns, besides metrical Psalms.]

    18. [RAm] The Church Hymnary. A Collection of Hymns and Tunes for Public Worship. Compiled by Edwin A. Bedell. [Adopted by the General Synod of the Reformed Church of North America.] New York. 1890. [994 hymns.]

    19. [RUS] The Hymnal of the Reformed Church in the United States. A selection of Hymns and Tunes for Christian Worship. Cleveland (Ohio). 1890. [760 hymns.]

    20. [RfE] Book of Common Praise. Hymnal Companion to the [Reformed Episcopal] Prayer-Book. Philadelphia. 1885. [541 hymns.]

    21. [UBr] Hymns for the Sanctuary and Social Worship, with Tunes. Dayton, Ohio: United Brethren Publishing House. 1874. [1234 hymns.]

---

    22. [BCh] The Sacrifice of Praise, with Tunes. Psalms, Hymns and Spiritual Songs designed for Public Worship and Private Devotion. [Edited by a Committee of the Session of the Brick Presbyterian Church.] New York. 1869. [616 hymns.]

    23. [Hat] The Church Hymn Book, with Tunes, for the Worship of God. Edited by Dr. Edwin F. Hatfield. New York. 1872. [1464 hymns.]

    24. [HES] Hymns and Songs of Praise for Public and Social Worship. Edited by Roswell D. Hitchcock, Zachary Eddy, Philip Schaff. New York. 1874. [1416 hymns.]

    25. [HEM] Carmina Sanctorum: a Selection of Hymns and Songs of Praise, with Tunes. Edited by Roswell Dwight Hitchcock, Zachary Eddy, Lewis Ward Mudge. New York. 1885. [746 hymns.]

    26. [HSP] Songs of Pilgrimage. A Hymnal for the Churches of Christ. By H. L. Hastings. Boston. 1886. [1533 hymns.]

    27. [H&L] The Evangelical Hymnal, with Tunes. Compiled by Rev. Charles Cuthbert Hall and Sigismond Lasar. New York. 1880. [610 hymns.]

    28. [LWB] The Church-Book. Hymns and Tunes for the Use of Christian Worship. Prepared by Leonard Woolsey Bacon. New York. 1883. [522 hymns.]

    29. [RSS] A Selection of Spiritual Songs, with Music for the Church and the Choir. Selected and arranged by Rev. Charles S. Robinson. New York. 1878-81. [1071 hymns.]

    30. [RLD.] Laudes Domini. A Selection of Spiritual Songs, Ancient and Modern. Edited by Rev. Charles S. Robinson. New York. 1884-87. [1168 hymns.]

The National Hymn Book.

YORK. C. M.
SCOTCH PSALTER, 1615.

1 Lord, it belongs not to my care
    Whether I die or live;
To love and serve Thee is my share,
    And this Thy grace must give.

2 If life be long, I will be glad
    That I may long obey;
If short, yet why should I be sad
    To soar to endless day?

3 Christ leads me through no darker rooms
    Than He went through before;
He that unto God's kingdom comes,
    Must enter by this door.

4 Come, Lord, when grace has made me meet
    Thy blessed face to see;
For if Thy work on earth be sweet,
    What will Thy glory be!

5 Then shall I end my sad complaints,
    And weary, sinful days,
And join triumphant with the saints
    Who sing Jehovah's praise.

6 My knowledge of that life is small;
    The eye of faith is dim;
But 'tis enough that Christ knows all,
    And I shall be with Him.

Rev. Richard Baxter, 1681.

BpC	664
BpN	438
BpS	1006
CoA	389
CoC	461
CoS	763
CoR	586
Dis	om
Ep	436
EAs	501
LuC	492
LuS	374
MEN	669
MES	om
Mor	1443
PrN	235
PrS	om
RAm	480
RUS	375
RfE	416
UBr	om
BCh	461
Hat	839
HES	1276
HEM	687
HSP	655
H&L	329
LWB	399
RSS	714
RLD	537

JERUSALEM. C. M. Double.

Modern Harp.

1 Jerusalem, my happy home,
  Name ever dear to me,
 When shall my labors have an end
  In joy and peace and thee?

2 When shall these eyes thy heaven-built walls
  And pearly gates behold?
 Thy bulwarks with salvation strong
  And streets of shining gold.

3 Oh, when, thou city of my God,
  Shall I thy courts ascend,
 Where congregations ne'er break up,
  And Sabbaths have no end?

4 There happier bowers than Eden bloom,
  Nor sin nor sorrow know;
 Blest seats, through rude and stormy scenes
  I onward press to you.

5 Why should I shrink at pain and woe,
  Or feel at death dismay?
 I've Canaan's goodly land in view
  And realms of endless day.

6 Jerusalem, my happy home,
  My soul still pants for thee;
 Then shall my labors have an end
  When I thy joys shall see.

F. B. P. Sixteenth Century.
David Dickson, ob. 1662.
Williams & Boden, 1801.

BpC 1048
BpN 682
BpS 1090
CoA 529
CoC 903
CoS 1231
CoR 624
Dis 643
Ep 496
EAs 855
LuC 579
LuS 590
MEN 1044
MES 560
Mor 183
PrN 790
PrS 668
RAm 977
RUS 55
RfE 493
UBr 1126

BCh 612
Hat 1442
HES 1372
HEM 703
HSP 1335
H&L 393
LWB 396
RSS 1292
RLD 1009

ST. STEPHEN. C. M.
Rev. WILLIAM JONES, 1780

1 Through all the changing scenes of life,
   In trouble and in joy,
The praises of my God shall still
   My heart and tongue employ.

2 Of His deliverance I will boast,
   Till all who are distressed
From my example comfort take,
   And charm their griefs to rest.

3 Oh, magnify the Lord with me,
   With me exalt His name!
When in distress to Him I called,
   He to my rescue came.

4 The hosts of God encamp around
   The dwellings of the just;
Deliverance He affords to all
   Who on His succor trust.

5 Oh, make but trial of His love:
   Experience will decide
How blest are they, and only they,
   Who in His truth confide.

6 Fear Him, ye saints, and ye will then
   Have nothing else to fear;
Make ye His service your delight:
   He'll make your wants His care.

             Rev. Nich. Brady, }
             Nahum Tate, } 1696.

BpC	197
BpN	83
BpS	202
CoA	451
CoC	429
CoR	om
CoS	230
Dis	om
Ep	415
EAs	om
LuC	86
LuS	om
MEN	om
MES	500
Mor	192
PrN	45
PrS	Ps34
RAm	629
RUS	382
RfE	395
UBr	om
BCh	64
Hnt	224
HES	142
HEM	455
HSP	1346
H&L	100
LWB	23
RSS	om
RLD	671

BARBY. C. M.
Wm. Tansur, 1735.

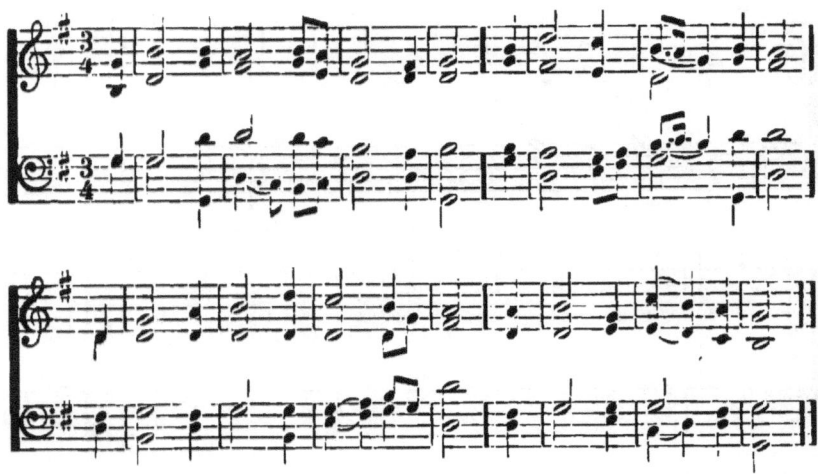

1. As pants the hart for cooling streams,
   When heated in the chase,
   So longs my soul, O God, for Thee,
   And Thy refreshing grace.

2. For Thee, my God, the living God,
   My thirsty soul doth pine;
   Oh, when shall I behold Thy face,
   Thou Majesty Divine?

3. Why restless, why cast down, my soul?
   Trust God, and He'll employ
   His aid for thee, and change these sighs
   To thankful hymns of joy.

4. God of my strength, how long shall I,
   Like one forgotten, mourn,
   Forlorn, forsaken, and exposed
   To my oppressor's scorn?

5. My heart is pierced, as with a sword,
   While thus my foes upbraid:
   "Vain boaster, where is now thy God?
   And where His promised aid?"

6. Why restless, why cast down, my soul?
   Hope still, and thou shalt sing
   The praise of Him who is thy God,
   Thy health's eternal Spring.

Tate and Brady, 1696.

BpC	608
BpN	380
BpS	223
CoA	om
CoC	451
CoS	654
CoR	om
Dis	66
Ep	451
EAs	585
LuC	om
LuS	402
MEN	550
MES	om
Mor	208
PrN	433
PrS	Ps42
RAm	599
RUS	444
RfE	om
UBr	660
BCh	395
Hat	870
HES	687
HEM	489
HSP	423
H&L	405
LWB	27
RSS	639
RLD	473

MORNING HYMN. L. M.
Dr. Wm. BOYCE, 1769.

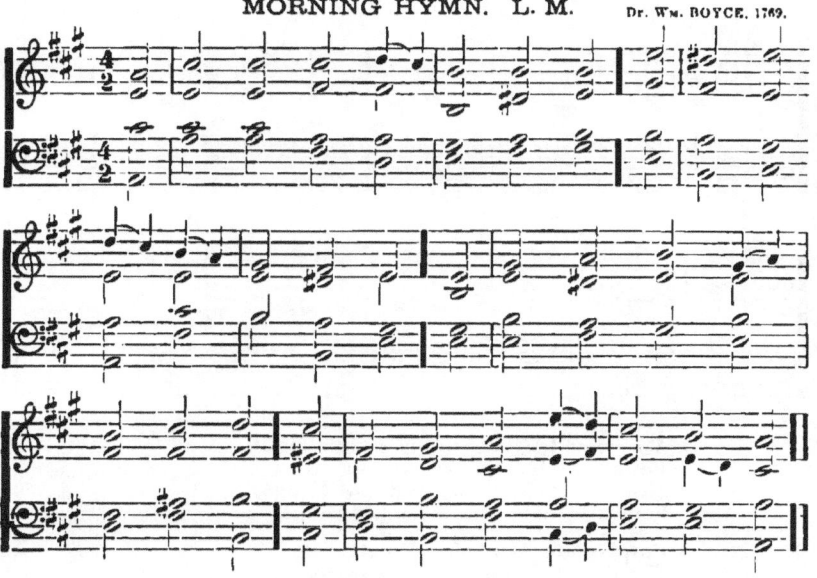

1 Awake, my soul, and with the sun
Thy daily stage of duty run;
Shake off dull sloth, and joyful rise
To pay thy morning sacrifice.

2 Wake and lift up thyself, my heart,
And with the angels bear thy part,
Who all night long unwearied sing
High praise to the eternal King.

3 All praise to Thee, Who safe hast kept,
And hast refreshed me whilst I slept!
Grant, Lord, when I from death shall wake,
I may of endless light partake!

4 Lord, I my vows to Thee renew;
Disperse my sins as morning dew;
Guard my first springs of thought and will,
And with Thyself my spirit fill.

5 Praise God from Whom all blessings flow,
Praise Him, all creatures here below!
Praise Him above, ye heavenly host;
Praise Father, Son and Holy Ghost!

BpC 80
BpN 49
BpS 30
CoA 550
CoC om
CoR 45
CoS 48
Dis 19
Ep 332
EAs 764
LuC 510
LuS 515
MEN 106
MES 749
Mor 356
PrN 890
PrS 438
RAm 827
RUS 622
RtE 252
UBr om
BCh 247
Hat 2
HES 1197
HEM 39
HSP 1529
H&L 9
LWB 472
RSS 9
RLD 48

Bishop Thomas Ken, 1695, 1709.

TALLIS'S CANON. L. M.
THOMAS TALLIS, 1565.

1. All praise to Thee, my God, this night,
   For all the blessings of the light;
   Keep me, O keep me, King of Kings,
   Beneath Thine own almighty wings!

2. Forgive me, Lord, for Thy dear Son,
   The ill that I this day have done,
   That with the world, myself and Thee,
   I, ere I sleep, at peace may be.

3. Teach me to live, that I may dread
   The grave as little as my bed!
   To die, that this vile body may
   Rise glorious at the awful day!

4. Oh may my soul on Thee repose;
   And may sweet sleep mine eyelids close;
   Sleep, that may me more vig'rous make
   To serve my God when I awake!

5. When in the night I sleepless lie,
   My soul with heavenly thoughts supply!
   Let no ill dreams disturb my rest,
   No powers of darkness me molest!

6. Oh when shall I, in endless day,
   Forever chase dark sleep away,
   And hymns with the supernal choir
   Incessant sing, and never tire?

7. Praise God from Whom all blessings flow,
   Praise Him all creatures here below!
   Praise Him above, ye heavenly host!
   Praise Father, Son and Holy Ghost!

   Bishop Thomas Ken, 1695, 1709.

BpC	85
BpN	57
BpS	33
CoA	562
CoC	71
CoR	46
CoS	65
Dis	258
Ep	333
EAs	769
LuC	522
LuS	519
MEN	105
MES	749
Mor	394
PrN	902
PrS	454
RAm	867
RUS	641
RfE	256
UBr	om
BCh	253
Hat	8
HES	1222
HEM	40
HSP	1533
H&L	16
LWB	475
RSS	154
RLD	113

MIGDOL. L. M.
LOWELL MASON, 1840.

1 Awake, our souls; away, our fears;
   Let every trembling thought be gone;
   Awake and run the heavenly race,
   And put a cheerful courage on.

2 True, 'tis a strait and thorny road,
   And mortal spirits tire and faint,
   But they forget the mighty God,
   That feeds the strength of every saint.

3 Thee, mighty God, whose matchless power
   Is ever new and ever young,
   And firm endures while endless years
   Their everlasting circles run,—

4 From Thee, the overflowing spring,
   Our souls shall drink a fresh supply,
   While such as trust their native strength
   Shall melt away, and droop, and die.

5 Swift as an eagle cuts the air,
   We'll mount aloft to Thine abode:
   On wings of love our souls shall fly,
   Nor tire amidst the heavenly road.

Dr. Isaac Watts, 1709.

BpC	734
BpN	410
BpS	952
CoA	407
CoC	624
CoR	349
CoS	890
Dis	om
Ep	473
EAs	om
LuC	459
LuS	85
MEN	om
MES	485
Mor	om
PrN	514
PrS	351
RAm	558
RUS	om
RfE	472
UBr	om
BCh	416
Hat	848
HES	655
HEM	om
HSP	cm
H&L	om
LWB	335
RSS	643
RLD	525

ST. THOMAS. S. M.
WM. TANSUR, 1768.

1 Come, we that love the Lord,
  And let our joys be known;
Join in a song with sweet accord,
  And thus surround the throne.

2 Let those refuse to sing
  Who never knew our God;
But fav'rites of the heavenly King
  May speak their joys abroad.

3 The men of grace have found
  Glory begun below;
Celestial fruits on earthly ground
  From faith and hope may grow.

4 The hill of Sion yields
  A thousand sacred sweets,
Before we reach the heavenly fields
  Or walk the golden streets.

5 Then let our songs abound
  And ev'ry tear be dry;
We're marching through Emmanuel's ground
  To fairer worlds on high.

Rev. Isaac Watts, 1709.

BpC	781
BpN	350
BpS	68
CoA	299
CoC	494
CoR	23
CoS	968
Dis	423
Ep	462
EAs	24
LuC	376
LuS	334
MEN	41
MES	484
Mor	1354
PrN	15
PrS	470
RAm	965
RUS	438
RfE	433
UBr	129
BCh	365
Hat	73
HES	607
HEM	34
HSP	587
H&L	50
LWB	om
RSS	42
RLD	31

WARWICK. C. M.   SAM. STANLEY, 1810.

1 Come, let us join our cheerful songs
   With angels round the throne ;
Ten thousand thousand are their tongues,
   But all their joys are one.

2 "Worthy the Lamb that died," they cry,
   "To be exalted thus!"
"Worthy the Lamb!" our lips reply,
   "For He was slain for us."

3 Jesus is worthy to receive
   Honor and power divine;
And blessings more than we can give
   Be, Lord, forever Thine.

4 Let all that dwell above the sky,
   And air, and earth, and seas,
Conspire to lift Thy glories high,
   And speak Thine endless praise.

5 The whole creation join in one
   To bless the sacred name
Of Him that sits upon the throne,
   And to adore the Lamb.

Dr. Isaac Watts, 1709.

BpC	279
BpN	166
BpS	453
CoA	150
CoC	209
CoR	329
CoS	338
Dis	43
Ep	208
EAs	12
LuC	164
LuN	160
MEN	2
MES	125
Mor	146
PrN	36
PrS	107
RAm	322
RUS	537
RfE	196
UBr	592
BCh	169
Hat	291
HES	330
HEM	236
HSP	1406
H&L	145
LWB	221
RSS	342
RLD	325

VARINA. C. M. Double.
C. H. BINCK, (Arr. by G. F. ROOT, 1849.)

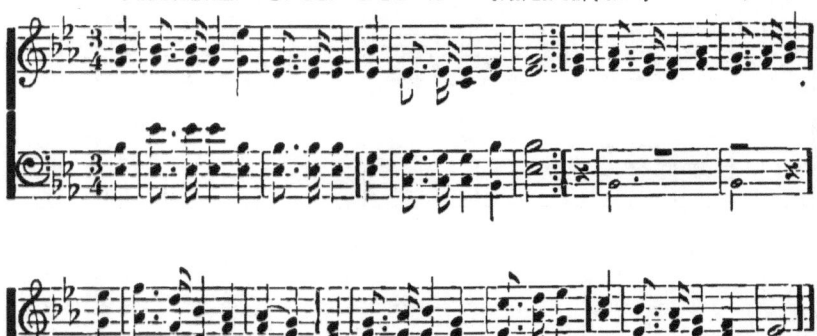

1 There is a land of pure delight,
    Where saints immortal reign;
  Infinite day excludes the night,
    And pleasures banish pain.

2 There everlasting spring abides,
    And never-withering flowers:
  Death, like a narrow sea, divides
    This heavenly land from ours.

3 Sweet fields, beyond the swelling flood,
    Stand dressed in living green;
  So to the Jews old Canaan stood,
    While Jordan rolled between.

4 But timorous mortals start and shrink
    To cross this narrow sea;
  And linger shivering on the brink,
    And fear to launch away.

5 Oh, could we make our doubts remove,
    Those gloomy doubts that rise,
  And see the Canaan that we love
    With unbeclouded eyes!—

6 Could we but climb where Moses stood,
    And view the landscape o'er,
  Not Jordan's stream, nor death's cold flood,
    Should fright us from the shore.

                    Rev. Isaac Watts, 1709.

BpC	1089
BpN	684
BpS	1066
CoA	527
CoC	900
CoR	612
CoS	1191
DIs	390
Ep	488
EAs	852
LuC	574
LuS	572
MEN	1037
MES	554
Mor	176
PrN	781
PrS	685
RAm	973
RUS	661
RfE	492
UBr	1116
BCh	600
Hat	1427
HES	1405
HEM	710
HSP	0m
H&L	524
LWB	394
RSS	1262
RLD	997

THATCHER. S. M.
G. F. HANDEL, 1732.

1 How beauteous are their feet
   Who stand on Zion's hill,
Who bring salvation on their tongues,
   And words of peace reveal!

2 How charming is their voice,
   How sweet the tidings are!
"Zion, behold thy Saviour King;
   He reigns and triumphs here."

3 How happy are our ears,
   That hear this joyful sound,
Which kings and prophets waited for,
   And sought, but never found.

4 How blessed are our eyes,
   That see this heavenly light!
Prophets and kings desired it long,
   But died without the sight.

5 The watchmen join their voice,
   And tuneful notes employ;
Jerusalem breaks forth in songs,
   And deserts learn the joy.

6 The Lord makes bare His arm
   Through all the earth abroad;
Let every nation now behold
   Their Saviour and their God.

                Rev. Isaac Watts, 1709.

BpC	861
BpN	555
BpS	1163
CoA	212
CoC	769
CoR	508
CoS	1062
Dis	426
Ep	44
EAs	643
LuC	285
LuS	198
MEN	821
MES	190
Mor	om
PrN	583
PrS	574
RAm	711
RUS	556
RfE	47
UBr	om
BCh	491
Hat	1139
HES	851
HEM	605
HSP	591
H&L	om
LWB	442
RSS	1028
RLD	749

MARLOW. C. M.
Arr. by LOWELL MASON, 1832.

1 When I can read my title clear
   To mansions in the skies,
 I bid farewell to every fear,
   And wipe my weeping eyes.

2 Should earth against my soul engage,
   And hellish darts be hurled,
 Then I can smile at Satan's rage,
   And face a frowning world.

3 Let cares like a wild deluge come,
   And storms of sorrow fall;
 May I but safely reach my home,
   My God, my heaven, my all,—

4 There shall I bathe my weary soul
   In seas of heavenly rest,
 And not a wave of trouble roll
   Across my peaceful breast.

Rev. Isaac Watts, 1709.

BpC 1059
BpN 491
BpS 1069
CoA 520
CoC 410
CoR 346
CoS 1200
Dis om
Ep 458
EAs 489
LuC 380
LuS 383
MEN 659
MES 517
Mor om
PrN 789
PrS 672
RAm 470
RUS 381
RfE 446
UBr 1118

BCh 602
Hat 835
HES 1403
HEM 405
HSP 409
H&L om
LWB 404
RSS 682
RLD 841

ROTHWELL. L. M. W. TANSUR, 1713.

1 Stand up, my soul! shake off thy fears,
　And gird the gospel armor on;
March to the gates of endless joy,
　Where Jesus, thy great Captain's gone.

2 Hell and thy sins resist thy course;
　But hell and sin are vanquished foes:
Thy Jesus nailed them to the cross,
　And sung the triumph when He rose.

3 Then let my soul march boldly on;
　Press onward to the heavenly gate:
There peace and joy eternal reign,
　And glitt'ring robes for conquerors wait.

4 There shall I wear a starry crown,
　And triumph in almighty grace,
While all the armies of the skies
　Join in my glorious Leader's praise.

Rev. Isaac Watts, 1709.

BpC	733
BpN	409
BpS	948
CoA	411
CoC	623
CoR	471
CoS	889
Dis	om
Ep	124
EAs	562
LuC	460
LuS	455
MEN	om
MES	522
Mor	398
PrN	515
PrS	394
RAm	556
RUS	om
RfE	om
UBr	757
BCh	474
Hat	847
HES	651
HEM	421
HSP	186
H&L	317
LWB	330
RSS	642
RLD	524

CAMBRIDGE. C. M.
JOHN RANDALL, 1790.

1 Salvation! oh, the joyful sound!
　'Tis pleasure to our ears!
　A sovereign balm for every wound,
　　A cordial for our fears.

2 Buried in sorrow and in sin,
　At hell's dark door we lay;
　But we arise, by grace divine,
　　To see a heavenly day.

3 Salvation! let the echo fly
　The spacious earth around,
　While all the armies of the sky
　　Conspire to raise the sound!

4 Salvation! O thou bleeding Lamb,
　To Thee the praise belongs:
　Our hearts shall kindle at Thy Name,
　　Thy Name inspire our songs.
　　　　　　Rev. Isaac Watts, 1709.

BpC 423
BpN 234
BpS 481
CoA 315
CoC 261
CoR om
CoS 106
Dis 53
Ep 369
EAs 193
LuC om
LuS 102
MEN 324
MES 130
Mor om
PrN 871
PrS 422
RAm 392
RUS 117
RfE 322
UBr om

BCh 280
Hat 558
HES 445
HEM om
HSP 1407
H&L om
LWB 317
RSS 458
RLD 569

ST. AGNES. C. M.
J. B. DYKES, 1864.

1 Come, Holy Spirit, heavenly Dove,
　With all Thy quickening powers;
　Kindle a flame of sacred love
　　In these cold hearts of ours.

2 Look, how we grovel here below,
　Fond of these trifling toys;
　Our souls can neither fly nor go
　　To reach eternal joys.

3 In vain we tune our formal songs,
　In vain we strive to rise;
　Hosannas languish on our tongues,
　　And our devotion dies.

4 Dear Lord, and shall we ever live
　At this poor dying rate,
　Our love so faint, so cold to Thee
　　And Thine to us so great?

5 Come, Holy Spirit, heavenly Dove,
　With all Thy quickening powers;
　Come, shed abroad a Saviour's love,
　　And that shall kindle ours.

　　　　　　　　　Dr. Isaac Watts, 1709.

BpC 366
BpN 196
BpS 521
CoA 188
CoC 221
CoR 142
CoS 462
Dis om
Ep 128
EAs 156
LuC 253
LuS 182
MEN 277
MES 153
Mor 142
PrN 76
PrS 137
RAm 363
RUS 331
RfE 128
UBr 363
BCh 179
Hat 314
HES 359
HEM 265
HSP 630
H&L 270
LWB 242
RSS 303
RLD 357

GRATITUDE. L. M.   AMI BOST, Arr. by T. HASTINGS, 1837.

1 My God, how endless is Thy love!
    Thy gifts are every evening new;
  And morning mercies, from above,
    Gently distill, like early dew.

2 Thou spread'st the curtains of the night,
    Great Guardian of my sleeping hours;
  Thy sovereign word restores the light,
    And quickens all my drowsy powers.

3 I yield my powers to Thy command;
    To Thee I consecrate my days:
  Perpetual blessings from Thy hand
    Demand perpetual songs of praise.
                    Rev. Isaac Watts, 1709.

BpC	83
BpN	50
BpS	om
CoA	om
CoC	65
CoR	48
CoS	62
Dis	182
Ep	324
EAs	om
LuC	om
LuS	512
MEN	104
MES	752
Mor	om
PrN	900
PrS	449
RAm	862
RUS	626
RfE	348
UBr	om
BCh	254
Hat	4
HES	1200
HEM	544
HSP	20
H&L	2
LWB	120
RSS	795
RLD	169

HAMBURG. L. M.
L. MASON, fr. GREGORIAN CHANT, 1825.

1 When I survey the wondrous cross
On which the Prince of Glory died,
My richest gain I count but loss,
And pour contempt on all my pride.

2 Forbid it, Lord, that I should boast,
Save in the death of Christ my God:
All the vain things that charm me most—
I sacrifice them to His blood.

3 See, from His head, His hands, His feet,
Sorrow and love flow mingled down!
Did e'er such love and sorrow meet,
Or thorns compose so rich a crown?

4 Were the whole realm of nature mine,
That were an offering far too small:
Love so amazing, so divine,
Demands my soul, my life, my all!

Rev. Isaac Watts, 1709.

BpC	248
BpN	442
BpS	330
CoA	99
CoC	181
CoR	185
CoS	316
Dis	254
Ep	83
EAs	119
LuC	183
LuS	127
MEN	211
MES	78
Mor	331
PrN	147
PrS	352
RAm	251
RUS	236
RfE	86
UBr	261
BCh	100
Hat	462
HES	245
HEM	197
HSP	50
H&L	231
LWB	188
RSS	312
RLD	275

LISBON. S. M.   DAN. READ, 1785.

1 Welcome, sweet day of rest,
   That saw the Lord arise!
 Welcome to this reviving breast,
   And these rejoicing eyes!

2 The King Himself comes near,
   And feasts His saints to-day;
 Here may we sit, and see Him here,
   And love, and praise, and pray.

3 One day, amidst the place
   Where my dear Lord hath been,
 Is sweeter than ten thousand days
   Of pleasure and of sin.

4 My willing soul would stay
   In such a frame as this,
 And sit and sing herself away
   To everlasting bliss.

                  Rev. Isaac Watts, D. D., 1709.

BpC	50
BpN	46
BpS	70
CoA	540
CoC	27
CoR	om
CoS	53
Dis	88
Ep	147
EAs	603
LuC	om
LuS	34
MEN	85
MES	234
Mor	1332
PrN	713
PrS	493
RAm	15
RUS	671
RfE	154
UBr	81
BCh	217
Hat	84
HES	934
HEM	84
HSP	529
H&L	33
LWB	480
RSS	43
RLD	43

BROWNELL. L.M. 61. Arr. fr. FR. JOS HAYDN.

1 The Lord my pasture shall prepare,
  And feed me with a shepherd's care;
  His presence shall my wants supply,
  And guard me with a watchful eye:
  My noon-day walks He shall attend,
  And all my midnight hours defend.

2 When in the sultry glebe I faint,
  Or on the thirsty mountain pant,
  To fertile vales, and dewy meads,
  My weary, wandering steps He leads;
  Where peaceful rivers, soft and slow,
  Amid the verdant landscape flow.

3 Though in the paths of death I tread,
  With gloomy horrors overspread,
  My steadfast heart shall fear no ill,
  For Thou, O Lord, art with me still:
  Thy friendly crook shall give me aid,
  And guide me through the dreadful shade.

4 Though in a bare and rugged way,
  Through devious, lonely wilds I stray,
  Thy presence shall my pains beguile:
  The barren wilderness shall smile,
  With sudden greens and herbage crown'd;
  And streams shall murmur all around.

            Joseph Addison, 1712.

BpC 204
BpN 73
BpS om
CoA 458
CoC 134
CoR 429
CoS 219
Dis 34
Ep 504
EAs 78
LuC 85
LuS 73
MEN 180
MES 30
Mor om
PrN 254
PrS Ps23
RAm 175
RUS om
RfE om
UBr om

BCh 58
Hat 821
HES 98
HEM 99
HSP om
H&L 375
LWB om
RSS 81
RLD 8

CREATION. L. M. 8 lines.
FRANCIS JOSEPH HAYDN, 1798.

CREATION. L. M. Concluded.

1 The spacious firmament on high,
   With all the blue ethereal sky,
   And spangled heavens, a shining frame,
   Their great Original proclaim.

2 Th' unwearied sun, from day to day,
   Does his Creator's power display,
   And publishes to every land
   The work of an Almighty hand.

3 Soon as the evening shades prevail,
   The moon takes up the wondrous tale,
   And nightly to the listening earth
   Repeats the story of her birth,

4 While all the stars that round her burn,
   And all the planets in their turn,
   Confirm the tidings as they roll,
   And spread the truth from pole to pole.

5 What though, in solemn silence, all
   Move round this dark, terrestrial ball?
   What though nor real voice or sound
   Amidst their radiant orbs be found?

6 In reason's ear they all rejoice,
   And utter forth a glorious voice;
   For ever singing, as they shine,
   "The hand that made us is Divine."

   Joseph Addison, 1712.

BpC	155
BpN	om
BpS	122
CoA	om
CoC	125
CoR	92
CoS	119
Dis	10
Ep	508
EAs	51
LuC	79
LuS	68
MEN	138
MES	28
Mor	om
PrN	344
PrS	om
RAm	144
RUS	om
RfE	308
UBr	175
BCh	51
Hat	174
HES	63
HEM	104
HSP	om
H&L	116
LWB	om
RSS	264
RLD	183

GENEVA. C. M.

J. COLE, 1805.

C. M.

1 When all Thy mercies, O my God,
   My rising soul surveys,
Transported with the view, I'm lost
   In wonder, love and praise!

2 Unnumbered comforts on my soul
   Thy tender care bestowed,
Before my infant heart conceived
   From whom those comforts flowed.

3 When, in the slippery paths of youth,
   With heedless step I ran,
Thine arm, unseen, conveyed me safe,
   And led me up to man.

4 When worn with sickness, oft hast Thou
   With health renewed my face;
And, when in sins and sorrows sunk,
   Revived my soul with grace.

5 Ten thousand thousand precious gifts
   My daily thanks employ;
Nor is the least a cheerful heart,
   That tastes those gifts with joys.

6 Through every period of my life
   Thy goodness I'll pursue;
And, after death, in distant world.
   The glorious theme renew.

7 Through all eternity to Thee
   A joyful song I'll raise:
But, oh! eternity's too short
   To utter all Thy praise.

                    Joseph Addison, 1712.

BpC	194
BpN	89
BpS	205
CoA	450
CoC	402
CoR	104
CoS	211
Dis	296
Ep	426
EAs	74
LuC	17
LuS	75
MEN	160
MES	684
Mor	186
PrN	429
PrS	423
RAm	125
RUS	409
RfE	396
UBr	om
BCh	67
Hat	225
HES	90
HEM	138
HSP	om
H&L	112
LWB	126
RSS	225
RLD	187

LEIGHTON. S. M.
H. W. GREATOREX, 1849.

1 O, bless the Lord, my soul!
   Let all within me join,
 And aid my tongue to bless His name,
   Whose favors are divine.

2 O, bless the Lord, my soul!
   Nor let His mercies lie
 Forgotten in unthankfulness,
   And without praises die.

3 'Tis He forgives thy sins;
   'Tis He relieves thy pain;
 'Tis He that heals thy sicknesses,
   And makes thee young again.

4 He crowns thy life with love,
   When ransomed from the grave;
 He who redeemed my soul from hell,
   Hath sovereign power to save.

5 He fills the poor with good;
   He gives the sufferers rest:
 The Lord hath judgments for the proud,
   And justice for th' oppressed.

6 His wondrous works and ways
   He made by Moses known;
 But sent the world His truth and grace
   By His beloved Son.

Rev. Isaac Watts, 1719.

BpC	200
BpN	17
BpS	231
CoA	om
CoC	130
CoR	119
CoS	223
Dis	448
Ep	413
EAs	om
LuC	73
LuS	2
MEN	749
MES	36
Mor	om
PrN	52
PrS	P103
RAm	118
RUS	631
RfE	408
UBr	29
BCh	16
Hat	237
HES	87
HEM	om
HSP	om
H&L	om
LWB	70
RSS	669
RLD	826

DARLEY. L. M.
W. H. DARLEY, d. 1872.

1 Sweet is the work, my God, my King.
  To praise Thy name, give thanks, and sing;
  To show Thy love by morning light,
  And talk of all Thy truth at night.

2 Sweet is the day of sacred rest;
  No mortal cares shall seize my breast:
  Oh, may my heart in tune be found,
  Like David's harp of solemn sound!

3 My heart shall triumph in my Lord,
  And bless His works, and bless His word;
  Thy works of grace, how bright they shine!
  How deep Thy counsels, how divine!

4 Fools never raise their thoughts so high,
  Like brutes they live, like brutes they die;
  Like grass they flourish, till Thy breath
  Blast them in everlasting death.

5 But I shall share a glorious part,
  When grace hath well refined my heart,
  And fresh supplies of joy are shed,
  Like holy oil, to cheer my head.

6 Then shall I see, and hear, and know
  All I desired or wished below;
  And every power find sweet employ
  In that eternal world of joy.

Rev. Isaac Watts, 1719.

BpC	57
BpN	12
BpS	15
CoA	546
CoC	2
CoR	om
CoS	11
Dis	267
Ep	150
EAs	600
LuC	46
LuS	43
MEN	81
MES	241
Mor	396
PrN	20
PrS	Ps92
RAm	31
RUS	om
Rf E	om
UBr	75
BCh	222
Hat	43
HES	944
HEM	79
HSP	92
H&L	86
LWB	59
RSS	6
RLD	43

WINDHAM. L. M.

DAN. READ, 1785.

1 O Thou that hear'st when sinners cry,
   Though all my crimes before Thee lie,
   Behold me not with angry look,
   But blot their memory from Thy book.

2 Create my nature pure within,
   And form my soul averse to sin;
   Let Thy good Spirit ne'er depart,
   Nor hide Thy presence from my heart.

3 I cannot live without Thy light,
   Cast out and banished from Thy sight;
   Thy holy joys, my God, restore,
   And guard me that I fall no more.

4 Though I have grieved Thy Spirit, Lord,
   His help and comfort still afford;
   And let a sinner seek Thy throne,
   To plead the merits of Thy Son.

5 A broken heart, my God, my King,
   Is all the sacrifice I bring:
   The God of grace will ne'er despise
   A broken heart for sacrifice.

6 My soul lies humbled in the dust,
   And owns Thy dreadful sentence just:
   Look down, O Lord, with pitying eye,
   And save the soul condemned to die.

7 Then will I teach the world Thy ways;
   Sinners shall learn Thy sovereign grace:
   I'll lead them to my Saviour's blood,
   And they shall praise a pardoning God.

8 Oh, may Thy love inspire my tongue!
   Salvation shall be all my song;
   And all my powers shall join to bless
   The Lord, my Strength and Righteousness.

Rev. Isaac Watts, 1719.

BpC	om
BpN	296
BpS	om
CoA	om
CoC	334
CoR	om
CoS	595
Dis	om
Ep	386
EAs	261
LuC	356
LuS	301
MEN	om
MES	298
Mor	om
PrN	295
PrS	756
RAm	om
RUS	167
RfE	356
UBr	501
BCh	320
Hat	610
HES	466
HEM	om
HSP	om
H&L	om
LWB	35
RSS	623
RLD	om

DUNDEE. C. M.   Scotch Psalter, 1615.

1 Our God, our help in ages past,
    Our hope for years to come,
  Our shelter from the stormy blast,
    And our eternal home!

2 Under the shadow of Thy throne,
    Thy saints have dwelt secure;
  Sufficient is Thine arm alone,
    And our defence is sure.

3 Before the hills in order stood,
    Or earth received her frame,
  From everlasting Thou art God,
    To endless years the same.

4 Thy word commands our flesh to dust:
    "Return, ye sons of men;"
  All nations rose from earth at first,
    And turn to earth again.

5 A thousand ages in Thy sight
    Are like an evening gone;
  Short as the watch that ends the night,
    Before the rising sun.

6 Time, like an ever-rolling stream,
    Bears all its sons away;
  They fly, forgotten, as a dream
    Dies at the opening day.

7 Our God, our help in ages past,
    Our hope for years to come,
  Be Thou our guard while troubles last,
    And our eternal home!

BpC 141
BpN 66
BpS 172
CoA 456
CoC 869
CoR 112
CoS 146
Dis 39
Ep 29
EAs 53
LuC 538
LuS 389
MEN 964
MES 527
Mor 126
PrN 435
PrS PsXC
RAm 126
RUS 379
RfE 30
UBr 1071

BCh 35
Hat 1338
HES 74
HEM 133
HSP 311
H&L 101
LWB 55
RSS 964
RLD 248

Rev. Isaac Watts, 1719.

ANTIOCH. C. M. G. F. HANDEL. Arr. by L. MASON, 1836.

1 Joy to the world! the Lord is come!
   Let earth receive her King;
   Let every heart prepare Him room,
   And heaven and nature sing.

2 Joy to the earth! the Saviour reigns!
   Let men their songs employ,
   While fields and floods, rocks, hills and plains
   Repeat the sounding joy.

3 No more let sins and sorrows grow,
   Nor thorns infest the ground;
   He comes to make His blessings flow
   Far as the curse is found.

4 He rules the earth with truth and grace,
   And makes the nations prove
   The glories of His righteousness
   And wonders of His love.

Rev. Isaac Watts, 1719.

BpC 209
BpN 105
BpS 231
CoA 42
CoC 163
CoR 157
CoS 277
Dis 72
Ep 40
EAs 82
LuC 134
LuS 110
MEN 183
MES 62
Mor 191
PrN 98
PrS Ps 98
RAm 206
RUS 44
RfE 17
UBr 200
BCh 84
Hat 391
HES 156
HEM 158
HSP om
H&L 191
LWB 65
RSS 236
RLD 322

DARWELL. H. M.
Rev. J. DARWELL, 1750.

1 Lord of the worlds above,
  How pleasant and how fair
The dwellings of Thy love,
  Thy earthly temples are!
    To Thine abode
      My heart aspires
      With warm desires
    To see my God.

2 The sparrow for her young
    With pleasure seeks a nest;
And wandering swallows long
    To find their wonted rest.
      My spirit faints
        With equal zeal
        To rise and dwell
      Among Thy saints.

3 O happy souls that pray
    Where God appoints to hear!
O happy men that pay
    Their constant service there!
      They praise Thee still;
        And happy they
        That love the way
      To Zion's hill.

4 They go from strength to strength,
    Through this dark vale of tears,
Till each arrives at length,
    Till each in heaven appears;
      O glorious seat,
        Where God our King
        Shall thither bring
      Our willing feet!

Rev. Isaac Watts, 1719.

BpC	19
BpN	38
BpS	om
CoA	22
CoC	16
CoR	16
CoS	om
Dis	148
Ep	157
EAs	om
LuC	43
LuS	48
MEN	15
MES	240
Mor	1168
PrN	579
PrS	Ps 84
RAm	11
RUS	362
RfE	158
UBr	146
BCh	189
Hat	65
HES	950
HEM	66
HSP	om
H&L	388
LWB	52
RSS	11
RLD	71

DUKE STREET. L. M.
J. HATTON, or WM. REEVE, 1790.

1 From all that dwell below the skies
  Let the Creator's praise arise;
  Let the Redeemer's name be sung
  Through every land, by every tongue.

2 Eternal are Thy mercies, Lord;
  Eternal truth attends Thy word:
  Thy praise shall sound from shore to shore,
  Till suns shall rise and set no more.
                    Rev. Isaac Watts, 1719.

BpC 139
BpN 6
BpS 1198
CoA 172
CoC 103
CoR 81
CoS 103
Dis 3
Ep 289
EAs 1
LuC 307
LuS 9
MEN 8
MES 605
Mor 314
PrN 5
PrS P117
RAm 142
RUS 668
RfE om
UBr 3

BCh 24
Hat 124
HES 50
HEM 103
HSP 69
H&L 88
LWB 75
RSS 96
RLD 82

MISSIONARY CHANT. L. M.
CHAS. ZEUNER, 1832.

1 Jesus shall reign where'er the sun
   Does his successive journeys run:
   His kingdom stretch from shore to shore,
   Till moons shall wax and wane no more.

2 For Him shall endless prayer be made,
   And praises throng to crown His head;
   His name, like sweet perfume, shall rise
   With every morning sacrifice.

3 Peoples and realms of every tongue
   Dwell on His love with sweetest song,
   And infant voices shall proclaim
   Their early blessings on His name.

4 Blessings abound where'er He reigns;
   The prisoner leaps to lose his chains;
   The weary find eternal rest,
   And all the sons of want are blest.

5 Where He displays His healing power,
   Death and the curse are known no more;
   In Him the tribes of Adam boast
   More blessings than their father lost.

6 Let every creature rise and bring
   Peculiar honors to our King;
   Angels descend with songs again,
   And earth repeat the loud Amen.

   Rev. Isaac Watts, 1719.

BpC 398
BpN 597
BpS 120
CoA 295
CoC 786
CoR 552
CoS 112
Dis 247
Ep 284
EAs 680
LuC 295
LuS 213
MEN 919
MES 609
Mor 303
PrN 175
PrS Ps72
RAm 795
RUS 109
RfE 298
UBr 895

BCh 123
Hat 1101
HES 1115
HEM 622
HSP 102
H&L 469
LWB 48
RSS 1141
RLD 911

NEWCOURT. L. P. M.
HUGH BOND, 1790.

1 I'll praise my Maker with my breath ;
And when my voice is lost in death,
   Praise shall employ my nobler powers:
My days of praise shall ne'er be past,
While life, and thought, and being last,
   Or immortality endures.

2 Happy the man whose hopes rely
On Israel's God: He made the sky,
   And earth and seas, with all their train:
His truth forever stands secure :
He saves the oppressed, He feeds the poor,
   And none shall find His promise vain.

3 The Lord hath eyes to give the blind ;
The Lord supports the sinking mind;
   He sends the laboring conscience peace:
He helps the stranger in distress,
The widow and the fatherless,
   And grants the prisoner sweet release.

4 I'll praise Him while He lends me breath ;
And when my voice is lost in death,
   Praise shall employ my nobler powers ;
My days of praise shall not be past,
While life, and thought, and being last,
   Or immortality endures.

Rev. Isaac Watts, 1719.

BpC	126
BpN	om
BpS	170
CoA	26
CoC	89
CoR	om
CoS	221
Dis	32
Ep	420
EAs	435
LuC	2
LuS	17
MEN	740
MES	48
Mor	om
PrN	55
PrS	P146
RAm	110
RUS	om
RfE	om
UBr	43
BCh	20
Hat	191
HES	4
HEM	122
HSP	900
H&L	102
LWB	96
RSS	om
RLD	90

ARLINGTON. C. M.
Dr. THOS. A. ARNE, 1762.

1 Am I a soldier of the cross?
   A follower of the Lamb?
And shall I fear to own His cause,
   Or blush to speak His name?

2 Must I be carried to the skies
   On flowery beds of ease,
While others fought to win the prize,
   And sailed through bloody seas?

3 Are there no foes for me to face?
   Must I not stem the flood?
Is this vile world a friend to grace,
   To help me on to God?

4 Sure I must fight if I would reign;
   Increase my courage, Lord!
I'll bear the toil, endure the pain,
   Supported by Thy word.

5 Thy saints in all this glorious war
   Shall conquer, though they die;
They see the triumph from afar,
   And seize it with their eye.

6 When that illustrious day shall rise,
   And all Thy armies shine
In robes of victory through the skies,
   The glory shall be Thine.

Rev. Isaac Watts, 1720.

BpC	736
BpN	417
BpS	720
CoA	410
CoC	626
CoR	885
CoS	481
Dis	625
Ep	471
EAs	563
LuC	461
LuS	456
MEN	598
MES	520
Mor	189
PrN	518
PrS	896
RAm	563
RUS	475
RfE	469
UBr	751
BCh	476
Hat	1052
HES	625
HEM	430
HSP	473
H&L	318
LWB	344
RSS	646
RLD	706

OLD HUNDREDTH. L. M.
Guillaume Franc, 1543.

1. Before Jehovah's awful throne,
    Ye nations, bow with sacred joy;
  Know that the Lord is God alone;
    He can create, and He destroy.

2. His sov'reign power, without our aid,
    Made us of clay, and formed us men;
  And when like wandering sheep we strayed,
    He brought us to His fold again.

3. We are His people, we His care—
    Our souls, and all our mortal frame:
  What lasting honors shall we rear,
    Almighty Maker, to Thy name?

4. We'll crowd Thy gates with thankful songs,
    High as the heavens our voices raise;
  And earth, with her ten thousand tongues,
    Shall fill Thy courts with sounding praise.

5. Wide as the world is Thy command,
    Vast as eternity Thy love:
  Firm as a rock Thy truth must stand,
    When rolling years shall cease to move.

Dr. Isaac Watts, 1719.
Rev. Charles Wesley, 1741.

BpC	2
BpN	5
BpS	117
CoA	14
CoC	127
CoR	85
CoS	33
Dis	1
Ep	409
EAs	2
LuC	1
LuS	1
MEN	9
MES	41
Mor	312
PrN	2
PrS	Ps C
RAm	141
RUS	663
RfE	400
UBr	1
BCh	11
Hat	165
HEM	101
HES	48
HSP	om
H&L	38
LWB	66
RSS	136
RLD	78

EL PARAN. L. M. CARMINA SACRA.

1 Another six days' work is done,
  Another Sabbath is begun;
  Return, my soul, enjoy thy rest,
  Improve the day thy God hath blessed.

2 Come, bless the Lord, whose love assigns
  So sweet a rest to wearied minds;
  Provides an antepast of heaven,
  And gives this day the food of seven.

3 O that our thoughts and thanks may rise,
  As grateful incense, to the skies;
  And draw from heaven that sweet repose,
  Which none but he that feels it knows.

4 This heavenly calm within the breast
  Is the dear pledge of glorious rest,
  Which for the church of God remains,
  The end of cares, the end of pains.

5 In holy duties, let the day,
  In holy pleasures, pass away;
  How sweet the Sabbath thus to spend,
  In hope of one that ne'er shall end!

Rev. Joseph Stennett, 1732.

BpC 58
BpN 42
BpS 22
CoA om
CoC 42
CoR 8
CoS 61
Dis om
Ep 153
EAs om
LuC 38
LuS 38
MEN om
MES 235
Mor om
PrN 701
PrS 423
RAm 34
RUS om
RfE 150
UBr 76
BCh 211
Hat 44
HES 940
HEM 78
HSP om
H&L om
LWB 441
RSS 47
RLD 12

SEASONS. L. M.
IGNAZ PLEYEL, 1831.

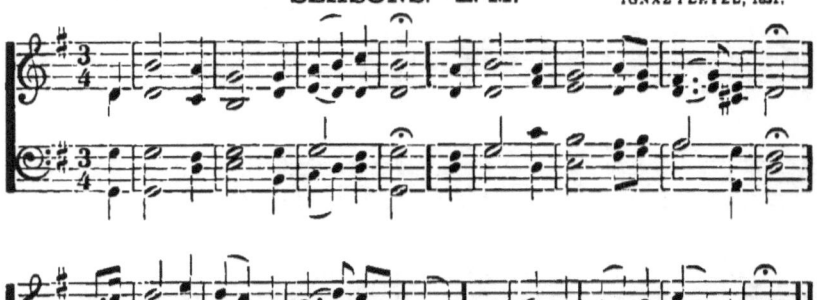

1 O Thou, to Whose all-searching sight
  The darkness shineth as the light,
  Search, prove my heart; it pants for Thee;
  O, burst these bonds, and set it free.

2 Wash out its stains, refine its dross;
  Nail my affections to the cross;
  Hallow each thought; let all within
  Be clean as Thou, my Lord, art clean.

3 While in this darksome wild I stray,
  Be Thou my light, be Thou my way:
  No foes, no violence I fear,
  No harm, while Thou, my God, art near.

4 When rising floods my soul o'erflow,
  When sinks my heart in waves of woe,
  Jesus, Thy timely aid impart,
  And raise my head, and cheer my heart.

5 Saviour, where'er Thy steps I see,
  Dauntless, untired, I follow Thee;
  Oh, let Thy hand support me still,
  And lead me to Thy holy hill!

6 If rough and thorny be the way,
  My strength proportion to the day;
  Till toil and grief and pain shall cease,
  Where all is calm and joy and peace.

Count Nich. Ludwig von Zinzendorf, 1721.
Rev. John Wesley, tr. 1739.

BpC	695
BpN	om
BpS	om
CoA	om
CoC	om
CoR	om
CoS	402
Dis	om
Ep	62
EAs	363
LuC	449
LuS	om
MEN	496
MES	489
Mor	om
PrN	188
PrS	307
RAm	om
RUS	185
RfE	52
UBr	om
BCh	431
Hat	927
HES	704
HEM	415
HSP	om
H&L	312
LWB	om
RSS	569
RLD	om

LOUVAN. L. M.
V. C. Taylor, 1849.

1 Jesus, Thy blood and righteousness
My beauty are, my glorious dress;
'Midst flaming worlds, in these arrayed,
With joy I shall lift up my head.

2 Bold shall I stand in Thy great day,
For who aught to my charge shall lay?
Fully absolved through these I am
From sin and fear, from guilt and shame.

3 When from the dust of death I rise
To claim my mansion in the skies,
E'en then this shall be all my plea:
Jesus hath lived, hath died for me.

4 Thus Abraham, the friend of God,
Thus all heaven's armies bought with blood,
Saviour of sinners Thee proclaim,
Sinners of whom the chief I am.

5 This spotless robe the same appears
When ruined nature sinks in years;
No age can change its glorious hue,
The robe of Christ is ever new.

6 Oh let the dead now hear Thy voice:
Bid, Lord, Thy mourning ones rejoice;
Their beauty this, their glorious dress,
Jesus the Lord our righteousness.

Count Zinzendorf, 1739.
Rev. John Wesley, 1740.

BpC	335
BpN	481
BpS	881
CoA	171
CoC	340
CoR	om
CoS	1003
Dis	om
Ep	480
EAs	301
LuC	372
LuS	321
MEN	238
MES	352
Mor	om
PrN	133
PrS	256
RAm	om
RUS	184
RfE	488
UBr	om
BCh	154
Hat	816
HES	om
HEM	331
HSP	87
H&L	om
LWB	om
RSS	927
RLD	607

MENDELSSOHN. 7s. D.　　J. L. F. MENDELSSOHN-BARTHOLDY, 1840.

7s. Double.

1. Hark! the herald angels sing
   Glory to the new-born King!
   Peace on earth, and mercy mild,
   God and sinners reconciled!
   Joyful, all ye nations, rise,
   Join the triumph of the skies;
   Universal nature say,
   Christ the Lord is born to-day.

2. Christ, by highest heaven adored;
   Christ the everlasting Lord;
   Late in time behold Him come,
   Offspring of a virgin's womb:
   Veiled in flesh the godhead see:
   Hail th' incarnate deity,
   Blessed as man with men t' appear,
   Jesus, our Immanuel here!

3. Hail! the heavenly Prince of Peace!
   Hail the Sun of Righteousness!
   Light and life to all He brings,
   Ris'n with healing in His wings.
   Mild He lays His glory by,
   Born that man no more may die,
   Born to raise the sons of earth,
   Born to give them second birth.

4. Come, desire of nations, come,
   Fix in us Thy humble home!
   Rise, the woman's conquering seed,
   Bruise in us the serpent's head!
   Now display Thy saving power,
   Ruined nature now restore,
   Now in mystic union join
   Thine to ours and ours to Thine!

5. Adam's likeness, Lord, efface;
   Stamp Thine image in its place;
   Second Adam from above,
   Reinstate us in Thy love!
   Let us Thee, though lost, regain;
   Thee the life, the heavenly man:
   O! to all Thyself impart,
   Formed in each believing heart!

Rev. Charles Wesley, 1739. Rev. Martin Madan, 1760.

BpC	224
BpN	188
BpS	272
CoA	45
CoC	167
CoR	164
CoS	270
Dis	130
Ep	17
EAs	om
LuC	128
LuS	230
MEN	190
MES	53
Mor	1074
PrN	114
PrS	om
RAm	182
RUS	61
RfE	19
UBr	219
BCh	om
Hat	403
HES	170
HEM	151
HSP	om
H&L	210
LWB	172
RSS	292
RLD	245

EASTER HYMN.

WILLIAM HENRY MONK.

1 Christ the Lord is risen to-day,
  Sons of men and angels say:
  Raise your joys and triumphs high,
  Sing, ye heavens, and earth reply.

2 Love's redeeming work is done,
  Fought the fight, the battle won:
  Lo! our Sun's eclipse is o'er;
  Lo! He sets in blood no more.

3 Vain the stone, the watch, the seal;
  Christ hath burst the gates of hell!
  Death in vain forbids His rise;
  Christ hath opened Paradise!

4 Lives again one glorious King:
  Where, O Death, is now thy sting?
  Once He died, our souls to save:
  Where thy victory, O Grave?

5 Soar we now where Christ has led,
  Following our exalted Head;
  Made like Him, like Him we rise:
  Ours the cross, the grave, the skies.

6 Hail the Lord of earth and heaven!
  Praise to Thee by both be given!
  Thee we greet triumphant now!
  Hail, the Resurrection Thou!

Rev. Chas. Wesley, 1749.

BpC	264
BpN	om
BpS	364
CoA	110
CoC	191
CoR	165
CoS	354
Dis	124
Ep	98
EAs	142
LuC	192
LuS	230
MEN	260
MES	99
Mor	46
PrN	155
PrS	om
RAm	295
RUS	259
RfE	101
UBr	322
BCh	106
Hat	474
HES	260
HEM	216
HSP	om
H&L	254
LWB	204
RSS	383
RLD	305

RATISBON. 7s. Rev. JOACHIM NEANDER.

1 Christ, whose glory fills the skies,
   Christ, the true, the only light,
  Sun of Righteousness, arise,
   Triumph o'er the shades of night;
  Day-spring from on high, draw near;
  Day-star, in my heart appear.

2 Dark and cheerless is the morn,
   Unaccompanied by Thee;
  Joyless is the day's return,
   Till Thy mercy's beams I see;
  Till Thou inward light impart,
  Glad my eyes and warm my heart.

3 Visit then this soul of mine;
   Pierce the gloom of sin and grief;
  Fill me, radiancy divine;
   Scatter all my unbelief:
  More and more Thyself display,
  Shining to the perfect day.
            Rev. Charles Wesley, 1740.

BpC 326
BpN om
BpS om
CoA 351
CoC 489
CoR om
CoS 425
Dis om
Ep 331
EAs 283
LuC 40
LuS 516
MEN 416
MES om
Mor 1271
PrN 896
PrS om
RAm 830
RvS 101
RfE 251
UBr om

BCh 128
Hat 897
HES 958
HEM 68
HSP 1129
H&L 55
LWB om
RSS 14
RLD 49

MARTYN. 7s. Double.

S. B. MARSH, 1836.

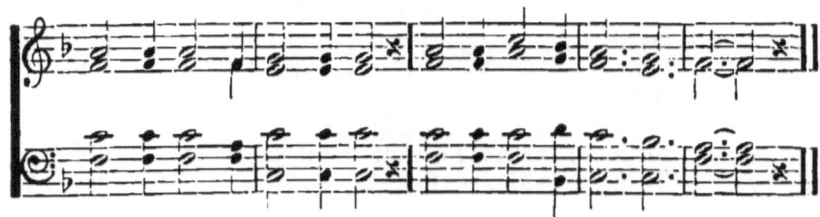

7s. Double.

1 Jesus, lover of my soul,
   Let me to Thy bosom fly,
While the nearer waters roll,
   While the tempest still is high!
Hide me, O my Saviour, hide
   Till the storm of life is past,
Safe into the haven guide;
   Oh receive my soul at last.

2 Other refuge have I none;
   Hangs my helpless soul on Thee;
Leave, ah! leave me not alone,
   Still support and comfort me:
All my trust on Thee is stayed,
   All my help from Thee I bring;
Cover my defenceless head
   With the shadow of Thy wing.

3 Wilt Thou not regard my call?
   Wilt Thou not accept my prayer?
Lo! I faint, I sink, I fall!
   Lo! on Thee I cast my care.
Reach me out Thy gracious hand!
   While I of Thy strength receive,
Hoping against hope I stand,
   Dying, and behold I live!

4 Thou, O Christ, art all I want,
   More than all in Thee I find:
Raise the fallen, cheer the faint,
   Heal the sick, and lead the blind.
Just and holy is Thy name,
   I am all unrighteousness;
False and full of sin I am,
   Thou art full of truth and grace.

5 Plenteous grace with Thee is found,
   Grace to cover all my sin:
Let the healing streams abound
   Make and keep me pure within.
Thou of life the fountain art;
   Freely let me take of Thee;
Spring Thou up within my heart,
   Rise to all eternity.

            Rev. Charles Wesley, 1740.

BpC	254
BpN	499
BpS	685
CoA	425
CoC	550
CoR	301
CoS	408
Dis	480
Ep	393
EAs	282
LuC	231
LuS	358
MEN	656
MES	334
Mor	1044
PrN	305
PrS	244
RAm	468
RUS	177
RfE	379
UBr	532
BCh	138
Hat	799
HES	676
HEM	450
HSP	726
H&L	155
LWB	155
RSS	605
RLD	505

PARK STREET. L. M.

F. M. A. VENUA, 1810.

1 Our Lord is risen from the dead,
   Our Jesus is gone up on high;
  The powers of hell are captive led,
   Dragged to the portals of the sky.

2 There His triumphal chariot waits,
   And angels chant the solemn lay:
  Lift up your heads, ye heavenly gates!
   Ye everlasting doors, give way!

3 Loose all your bars of massy light,
   And wide unfold th' ethereal scene:
  He claims these mansions as his right;
   Receive the King of glory in.

4 Who is the King of glory—who?
   The Lord who all our foes o'ercame;
  Who sin, and death, and hell o'erthrew;
   And Jesus is the Conqueror's name.

5 Lo! His triumphal chariot waits,
   And angels chant the solemn lay;
  Lift up your heads, ye heavenly gates!
   Ye everlasting doors, give way!

6 Who is the King of glory—who?
   The Lord, of boundless power possessed;
  The King of saints and angels, too,
   God over all, for ever blessed.

                     Rev. Chas. Wesley, 1741.

BpC	276
BpN	144
BpS	372
CoA	120
CoC	188
CoR	om
CoS	362
Dis	192
Ep	117
EAs	om
LuC	199
LuS	245
MEN	237
MES	98
Mor	934
PrN	151
PrS	om
RAm	301
RUS	311
RfE	122
UBr	316
BCh	113
Hat	486
HES	280
HEM	217
HSP	80
H&L	om
LWB	213
RSS	333
RLD	339

SEYMOUR. 7s.
C. M Von WEBER, 1825.

1 Sinners, turn; why will ye die?
God, your Maker, asks you why;
God Who did your being give,
Made you with Himself to live.

2 Sinners, turn; why will ye die?
God, your Saviour, asks you why;
Will ye not in Him believe?
He has died that ye might live.

3 Will ye let Him die in vain?
Crucify your Lord again?
Why, ye ransomed sinners, why
Will ye slight His grace, and die?

4 Sinners, turn; why will ye die?
God, the Spirit, asks you why—
He, Who all your lives hath strove,
Wooed you to embrace His love.

5 Will ye not His grace receive?
Will ye still refuse to live?
O ye dying sinners, why,
Why will ye forever die?

Rev. Charles Wesley, 1741.

BpC 463
BpN 264
BpS 611
CoA 322
CoC 312
CoR 254
CoS 539
Dis 649
Ep 54
EAs 248
LuC om
LuS 289
MEN 347
MES 261
Mor 1046
PrN 557
PrS 189
RAm 403
RUS om
RfE 345
UBr om

BCh 308
Hat 594
HES 416
HEM om
HSP 1117
H&L 278
LWB 460
RSS 492
RLD 591

EVAN. C. M.   Rev. W. H. HAVERGAL, 1849.

1 Oh for a heart to praise my God!
   A heart from sin set free;
   A heart that's sprinkled with the blood
   So freely shed for me;—

2 A heart resigned, submissive, meek,
   My dear Redeemer's throne;
   Where only Christ is heard to speak,
   Where Jesus reigns alone.

3 A humble, lowly, contrite heart,
   Believing, true, and clean;
   Which neither life nor death can part
   From Him that dwells within!

4 A heart in every thought renewed,
   And full of love divine;
   Perfect, and right, and pure, and good,
   A copy, Lord, of Thine.

5 Thy nature, gracious Lord, impart;
   Come quickly from above;
   Write Thy new name upon my heart,
   Thy new, best name of Love.

                      Rev. Charles Wesley, 1742.

BpC	602
BpN	878
BpS	911
CoA	om
CoC	455
CoR	338
CoS	577
Dis	629
Ep	467
EAs	370
LuC	399
LuS	323
MEN	521
MES	408
Mor	116
PrN	410
PrS	318
RAm	598
RUS	478
RfE	461
UBr	645
BCh	425
Hat	936
HES	741
HEM	485
HSP	358
H&L	386
LWB	307
RSS	489
RLD	702

LUTHER. S. M.   THOMAS HASTINGS, 1835.

1 Lord of the harvest! hear
   Thy needy servants' cry;
Answer our faith's effectual prayer,
   And all our wants supply.

2 On Thee we humbly wait;
   Our wants are in Thy view;
The harvest, truly, Lord! is great,
   The laborers are few.

3 Convert and send forth more
   Into Thy church abroad,
And let them speak Thy word of power,
   As workers with their God.

4 Oh! let them spread Thy name,
   Their mission fully prove;
Thy universal grace proclaim,—
   Thine all-redeeming love.

Rev. Charles Wesley, 1742.

BpC	om
BpN	om
BpS	1165
CoA	om
CoC	768
CoR	om
CoS	om
Dis	om
Ep	170
EAs	om
LuC	288
LuS	222
MEN	818
MES	193
Mor	1199
PrN	om
PrS	815
RAm	710
RUS	557
RfE	294
UBr	1013
BCh	om
Hat	1138
HES	855
HEM	om
HSP	553
H&L	om
LWB	om
RSS	750
RLD	017

LEBANON. S. M. Double. JOHN ZUNDEL, 1855.

1 Jesus, my strength, my hope,
  On Thee I cast my care,
With humble confidence look up,
  And know Thou hearest my prayer.
Give me on Thee to wait,
  Till I can all things do;
On Thee, almighty to create,
  Almighty to renew.

2 I want a sober mind,
  A self-renouncing will,
That tramples down and leaves behind
  The baits of pleasing ill;
A soul inured to pain,
  To hardship, grief and loss,
Bold to take up, firm to sustain
  The consecrated cross.

3 I want a godly fear,
  A quick-discerning eye,
That looks to Thee when sin is near,
  And sees the tempter fly;
A spirit still prepared,
  And armed with jealous care,
Forever standing on its guard,
  And watching unto prayer.

4 I rest upon Thy word;
  The promise is for me;
My succor and salvation, Lord,
  Shall surely come from Thee.
But let me still abide
  Nor from my hope remove,
Till Thou my patient spirit guide
  Into Thy perfect love.

Rev. Charles Wesley, 1742.

BpC 731
BpN 386
BpS om
CoA om
CoC om
CoR 390
CoS om
Dis 458
Ep 434
EAs 379
LuC 401
LuS 353
MEN 505
MES 726
Mor om
PrN 180
PrS 321
RAm 487
RUS om
RfE 454
UBr 684

BCh 427
Hat 925
HES 751
HEM 495
HSP om
H&L 161
LWB 349
RSS 819
RLD 830

HARWELL. 8s & 7s. L. MASON, 1840.

1 Come, Thou long-expected Jesus,
  Born to set Thy people free;
From our fears and sins release us,
  Let us find our rest in Thee.
Israel's strength and consolation,
  Hope of all the earth Thou art;
Dear desire of every nation,
  Joy of every longing heart.

2 Born Thy people to deliver,
  Born a child and yet a King,
Born to reign in us forever,
  Now Thy gracious kingdom bring;
By Thine own eternal Spirit
  Rule in all our hearts alone;
By Thine all-sufficient merit
  Raise us to Thy glorious throne.

Rev. Charles Wesley, 1744.

BpC 217
BpN 107
BpS 276
CoA 43
CoC 1210
CoR om
CoS 894
Dis om
Ep 16
EAs om
LuC 126
LuS om
MEN 334
MES 735
Mor om
PrN 112
PrS 41
RAm 199
RUS om
RfE 16
UBr 224

BCh 90
Hat 411
HES 165
HEM 173
HSP 811
H&L 178
LWB 168
RSS 1103
RLD 756

FABEN. 8s, 7s. D.   Dr. J. H. WILCOX, 1849.

FABEN. 8s, 7s. D. Concluded.

1 Light of those whose dreary dwelling
　Borders on the shades of death,
Come, and by Thyself revealing,
　Dissipate the clouds beneath:
The new heaven and earth's Creator,
　In our deepest darkness rise,
Scattering all the night of nature,
　Pouring eye-sight on our eyes.

2 Still we wait for Thine appearing;
　Life and joy Thy beams impart,
Chasing all our fears, and cheering
　Every poor benighted heart:
Come and manifest the favor
　God hath for our ransomed race;
Come, Thou glorious God and Saviour,
　Come, and bring the gospel-grace.

3 Save us in Thy great compassion,
　O Thou mild pacific Prince!
Give the knowledge of salvation,
　Give the pardon of our sins;
By Thine all-restoring merit
　Every burdened soul release,
Every weary, wandering spirit
　Guide into Thy perfect peace.

　　　　　　Rev. Charles Wesley, 1745.

BpC 902
BpN 567
BpS om
CoA 157
CoC 533
CoR 225
CoS 426
Dis om
Ep 39
EAs om
LuC 125
LuS om
MEN 943
MES om
Mor 943
PrN 319
PrS om
RAm 348
RUS 24
RfE 49
UBr om

BCh 127
Hat 1201
HES 346
HEM 270
HSP 839
H&L 180
LWB 158
RSS 755
RLD 488

LOVE DIVINE. 8s, 7s. D.
JOHN ZUNDEL.

8s, 7s. Double.

1 Love Divine, all loves excelling,
    Joy of heaven, to earth come down,
Fix in us Thy humble dwelling,
    All Thy faithful mercies crown:
Jesus! Thou art all compassion,
    Pure, unbounded love Thou art;
Visit us with Thy salvation,
    Enter every trembling heart.

2 Breathe, oh breathe Thy loving Spirit
    Into every troubled breast!
Let us all in Thee inherit,
    Let us find that second rest.
Take away the love of sinning;
    Alpha and Omega be,—
End of faith as its beginning,
    Set our hearts at liberty.

3 Come, almighty to deliver!
    Let us all Thy life receive;
Suddenly return, and never,
    Never more Thy temples leave.
Thee we would be always blessing,
    Serve Thee as Thy hosts above;
Pray and praise Thee without ceasing,
    Glory in Thy perfect love.

4 Finish then Thy new creation;
    Pure and spotless let us be:
Let us see our whole salvation
    Perfectly secured by Thee!
Changed from glory into glory,
    Till in heaven we take our place,
Till we cast our crown before Thee,
    Lost in wonder, love and praise.

                Rev. Charles Wesley, 1746.

BpC	591
BpN	369
BpS	513
CoA	395
CoC	532
CoR	369
CoS	997
Dis	517
Ep	456
EAs	383
LuC	31
LuS	350
MEN	491
MES	411
Mor	948
PrN	314
PrS	315
RAm	584
RUS	102
RtE	121
UBr	701
BCh	393
Hat	393
HES	347
HEM	269
HSP	1256
H&L	121
LWB	348
RSS	760
RLD	566

SILVER STREET. S. M.

ISAAC SMITH, 1770.

1 Soldiers of Christ! arise,
   And put your armor on,—
Strong in the strength which God supplies
   Through His eternal Son.

2 Strong in the Lord of hosts,
   And in His mighty power:
Who in the strength of Jesus trusts,
   Is more than conqueror.

3 Stand, then, in His great might,
   With all His strength endued;
And take, to arm you for the fight,
   The panoply of God.

4 That, having all things done,
   And all your conflicts past,
Ye may o'ercome, through Christ alone,
   And stand entire at last.

5 Leave no unguarded place,
   No weakness of the soul;
Take every virtue, every grace,
   And fortify the whole.

6 Indissolubly joined,
   To battle all proceed;
But arm yourselves with all the mind
   That was in Christ your head.

          Rev. Charles Wesley, 1749.

BpC	747
BpN	424
BpS	962
CoA	258
CoC	617
CoR	om
CoS	898
Dis	417
Ep	216
EAs	572
LuC	462
LuS	454
MEN	587
MES	521
Mor	1498
PrN	666
PrS	416
RAm	565
RUS	462
RfE	185
UBr	761
BCh	475
Hat	1260
HES	628
HEM	423
HSP	561
H&L	319
LWB	om
RSS	579
RLD	om

ITALIAN HYMN. 6s & 4s. FELICE GIARDINI, 1760.

1 Come, Thou almighty King,
    Help us Thy name to sing,
        Help us to praise:
    Father, all-glorious,
    O'er all victorious,
    Come and reign over us,
        Ancient of Days!

2 Come, Thou incarnate Word!
    Gird on Thy mighty sword;
        Our prayer attend:
    Come and Thy people bless,
    And give Thy word success;
    Spirit of holiness,
        On us descend.

3 Come, Holy Comforter!
    Thy sacred witness bear
        In this glad hour:
    Thou, Who almighty art,
    Now rule in every heart,
    And ne'er from us depart,
        Spirit of power!

4 To the great One and Three
    The highest praises be
        Hence evermore!
    Thy sovereign majesty
    May we in glory see,
    And to eternity
        Love and adore.

Rev. Charles Wesley, 1757.

BpC 108
BpN 28
BpS 114
CoA 5
CoC 239
CoR 122
CoS 474
Dis om
Ep 428
EAs 32
LuC 30
LuS 66
MEN 6
MES 485
Mor 1234
PrN 847
PrS 459
RAm 92
RUS 448
RfE 143
UBr 394

BCh 3
Hat 158
HES 2
HEM 21
HSP 1173
H&L 43
LWB 99
RSS 122
RLD 223

55

TAMWORTH. 8s, 7s & 4s. CHAS. LOCKHART, 1790.

1 Lo! He comes, with clouds descending,
   Once for favored sinners slain;
   Thousand thousand saints, attending,
   Swell the triumph of His train:
      Hallelujah!
   Jesus shall forever reign.

2 Every eye shall now behold Him,
   Robed in dreadful majesty:
   Those who set at nought and sold Him,
   Pierced, and nailed Him to the tree,
      Deeply wailing,
   Shall the true Messiah see.

3 When the solemn trump has sounded,
   Heaven and earth shall flee away;
   All who hate Him must, confounded,
   Hear the summons of that day—
      "Come to judgment!—
   Come to judgment!—come away!"

4 Now the Saviour, long expected,
   See, in solemn pomp, appear;
   All His saints, by men rejected,
   Now shall meet Him in the air:
      Hallelujah!
   See the day of God appear.

5 Yea, amen; let all adore Thee,
   High on Thine eternal throne;
   Saviour, take the power and glory;
   Claim the kingdom for Thine own:
      Oh come quickly,
   Hallelujah! come, Lord, come.

Rev. John Cennick, 1750.   Rev. Charles Wesley, 1758.   Rev. Martin Madan, 1760.

```
BpC  1026
BpN   658
BpS   396
CoA   169
CoC   883
CoR   om
CoS   om
Dis   534
Ep      1
EAs   837
LuC   om
LuS   566
MEN  1013
MES   113
Mor   om
PrN   725
PrS   663
RAm   958
RUS    14
RfE     1
UBr   om

BCh   589
Hat  1401
HES  1340
HEM   699
HSP   814
H&L   om
LWB   om
RSS  1246
RLD   om
```

BROWN. C. M.
Wm. B. Bradbury, 1840.

1 Come let us join our friends above,
    That have obtained the prize,
  And on the eagle wings of love
    To joys celestial rise:

2 Let all the saints terrestrial sing
    With those to glory gone;
  For all the servants of our King,
    In earth and heaven are one.

3 One family we dwell in Him,
    One church above, beneath,
  Though now divided by the stream,
    The narrow stream of death.

4 One army of the living God,
    To His command we bow;
  Part of His host have crossed the flood,
    And part are crossing now.

5 Ten thousand to their endless home
    This solemn moment fly;
  And we are to the margin come,
    And we expect to die.

6 Oh that we now might grasp our Guide!
    Oh that the word were given!
  Come, Lord of hosts, the waves divide,
    And land us all in heaven!

Rev. Charles Wesley, 1759.

BpC	938
BpN	464
BpS	769
CoA	314
CoC	om
CoR	om
CoS	om
Dis	640
Ep	188
EAs	630
LuC	283
LuS	om
MEN	1033
MES	578
Mor	143
PrN	594
PrS	300
RAm	767
RUS	429
RfE	161
UBr	896
BCh	404
Hat	1172
HES	916
HEM	om
HSP	om
H&L	507
LWB	om
RSS	om
RLD	om

KENTUCKY. S. M.
AARON CHAPIN, 1822.

1 A charge to keep I have,
   A God to glorify,
 A never-dying soul to save,
   And fit it for the sky.

2 To serve the present age,
   My calling to fulfill;
 Oh may it all my powers engage,
   To do my Master's will!

3 Arm me with jealous care,
   As in Thy sight to live;
 And O! Thy servant, Lord, prepare
   A strict account to give.

4 Help me to watch and pray,
   And on Thyself rely;
 Assured, if I my trust betray,
   I shall forever die.

Rev. Charles Wesley, 1762.

BpC	749
BpN	454
BpS	926
CoA	251
CoC	574
CoR	456
CoS	916
Dis	432
Ep	474
EAs	565
LuC	457
LuS	428
MEN	574
MES	457
Mor	1340
PrN	456
PrS	385
RAm	566
RUS	456
RfE	om
UBr	798
BCh	411
Hat	922
HES	631
HEM	426
HSP	1401
H&L	320
LWB	369
RSS	397
RLD	561

PLEYEL'S HYMN. 7s.

IGNAZ PLEYEL, 1831.

1 Children of the heavenly King,
As ye journey, sweetly sing:
Sing your Saviour's worthy praise,
Glorious in His works and ways!

2 We are travelling home to God,
In the way the fathers trod;
They are happy now; and we
Soon their happiness shall see.

3 O ye banished seed, be glad!
Christ our advocate is made;
Us to save, our flesh assumes;
Brother to our souls becomes.

4 Shout, ye little flock, and blest!
You on Jesus' throne shall rest;
There your seat is now prepared,
There your kingdom and reward.

5 Fear not, brethren; joyful stand
On the borders of your land;
Jesus Christ, the Father's Son,
Bids you undismayed go on.

6 Lord, obediently we go,
Gladly leaving all below;
Only Thou our leader be,
And we still will follow Thee.

Rev. John Cennick, 1742.

BpC 776
BpN 359
BpS 967
CoA 298
CoC 611
CoR 363
CoS om
Dis om
Ep 449
EAs 461
LuC 379
LuS 444
MEN 720
MES 430
Mor 75
PrN 87
PrS 420
RAm 492
RUS 482
RfE 405
UBr 612

BCh 468
Hat 900
HES 585
HEM 389
HSP 1111
H&L 367
LWB 384
RSS 532
RLD 743

AMSTERDAM. 7s & 6s.

JAMES NARES, 1780.

1 Rise, my soul! and stretch thy wings,
  Thy better portion trace:
Rise, from transitory things,
  Toward heaven, thy native place:
Sun, and moon, and stars decay,
  Time shall soon this earth remove;
Rise, my soul, and haste away
  To seats prepared above!

2 Rivers to the ocean run,
  Nor stay in all their course;
Fire, ascending, seeks the sun,—
  Both speed them to their source;
So a soul that's born of God
  Pants to view His glorious face,
Upward tends to His abode,
  To rest in His embrace.

3 Cease, ye pilgrims! cease to mourn,—
  Press onward to the prize;
Soon your Saviour will return
  Triumphant in the skies:
Yet a season, and you know
  Happy entrance will be given,
All your sorrows left below,
  And earth exchanged for heaven.

Rev. Robert Seagrave, 1742.

BpC 1029
BpN 388
BpS 1037
CoA 598
CoC 914
CoR 560
CoS 1238
Dis om
Ep 447
EAs om
LuC 452
LuS 407
MEN 1068
MES 428
Mor 1473
PrN 797
PrS 671
RAm 602
RUS 468
RfE 443
UBr om

BCh 608
Hat 907
HES 726
HEM 409
HSP 986
H&L 385
LWB 393
RSS 1275
RLD 939

FERGUSON. S. M.
GEO. KINGSLEY, 1843.

1 Awake, and sing the song
    Of Moses and the Lamb!
  Wake, every heart, and every tongue,
    To praise the Saviour's name!

2 Sing of His dying love;
    Sing of His rising power,
  Sing how He intercedes above
    For those whose sins He bore.

3 Sing, till we feel our hearts
    Ascending with our tongues;
  Sing, till the love of sin departs,
    And grace inspires our songs.

4 Sing on your heavenly way,
    Ye ransomed sinners, sing!
  Sing on, rejoicing every day
    In Christ, th' exalted King.

5 Soon shall we hear Him say,
    "Ye blessed children, come!"
  Soon will He call us hence away
    And take His wanderers home.

Rev. William Hammond, 1745.

BpC	351
BpN	158
BpS	483
CoA	144
CoC	203
CoR	om
CoS	331
Dis	79
Ep	463
EAs	25
LuC	om
LuS	12
MEN	4
MES	483
Mor	1298
PrN	14
PrS	115
RAm	531
RUS	394
RfE	432
UBr	350
BCh	166
Hat	510
HES	606
HEM	353
HSP	590
H&L	127
LWB	386
RSS	32
RLD	36

CHESTERFIELD. C. M.
Rev. THOS. HAWEIS, 1792.

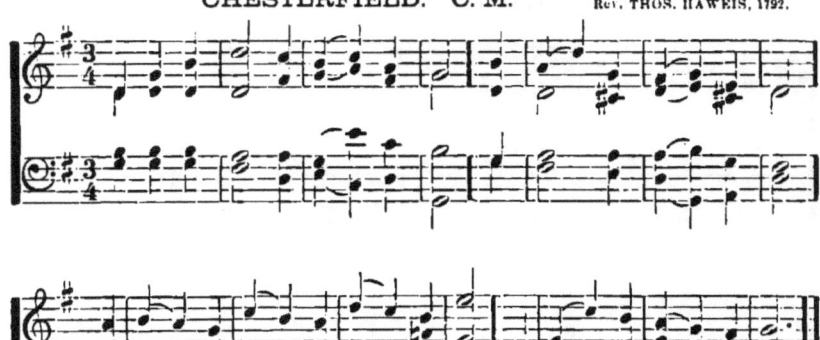

1 Hark the glad sound! the Saviour comes,
　The Saviour promised long;
　Let every heart prepare a throne,
　And every voice a song.

2 On Him the Spirit, largely poured,
　Exerts its sacred fire;
　Wisdom and might and zeal and love
　His holy breast inspire.

3 He comes the prisoners to release,
　In Satan's bondage held;
　The gates of brass before Him burst,
　The iron fetters yield.

4 He comes, from thickest films of vice
　To clear the mental ray,
　And on the eye-balls of the blind
　To pour celestial day.

5 He comes, the broken heart to bind,
　The bleeding soul to cure,
　And with the treasures of His grace
　T' enrich the humble poor.

6 Our glad Hosannas, Prince of Peace,
　Thy welcome shall proclaim,
　And heaven's eternal arches ring
　With Thy beloved name.

Rev. Philip Doddridge, 1735, 1755.

BpC	208
BpN	184
BpS	284
CoA	41
CoC	161
CoR	om
CoS	274
Dis	392
Ep	15
EAs	83
LuC	123
LuS	111
MEN	185
MES	52
Mor	195
PrN	99
PrS	70
RAm	203
RUS	52
RfE	2
UBr	202
BCh	88
Hat	392
HES	155
HEM	149
HSP	om
H&L	186
LWB	169
RSS	253
RLD	om

MANOAH. C. M.
ISAAC ROSSINI, 1868.

1 O God of Bethel! by whose hand
   Thy people still are fed;
Who through this weary pilgrimage
   Hast all our fathers led;—

2 Our vows, our prayers, we now present
   Before Thy throne of grace;
God of our fathers! be the God
   Of their succeeding race.

3 Through each perplexing path of life
   Our wandering footsteps guide;
Give us, each day, our daily bread,
   And raiment fit provide.

4 Oh spread Thy covering wings around,
   Till all our wanderings cease,
And at our Father's loved abode
   Our souls arrive in peace.

5 Such blessings from Thy gracious hand
   Our humble prayers implore;
And Thou shalt be our chosen God,
   Our portion evermore.

        Rev. Philip Doddridge, 1736, 1755.
        Rev. Mich. Bruce, 1745, 1781

BpC	196
BpN	om
BpS	198
CoA	om
CoC	411
CoR	339
CoS	216
Dis	311
Ep	826
EAs	om
LuC	91
LuS	86
MEN	om
MES	509
Mor	om
PrN	441
PrS	472
RAm	670
RUS	446
RfE	om
UBr	om
BCh	70
Hat	941
HES	1172
HEM	402
HSP	om
H&L	349
LWB	137
RSS	808
RLD	952

SILVER STREET. S. M.
ISAAC SMITH, 1770.

1 Grace! 'tis a charming sound,
   Harmonious to the ear;
Heaven with the echo shall resound,
   And all the earth shall hear.

2 Grace first contrived the way
   To save rebellious man;
And all the steps that grace display,
   Which drew the wondrous plan.

3 Grace taught my wandering feet
   To tread the heavenly road;
And new supplies each hour I meet,
   While pressing on to God.

4 Grace all the work shall crown
   Through everlasting days;
It lays in heaven the topmost stone,
   And well deserves the praise.

Rev. Philip Doddridge, 1755.

BpC	436
BpN	93
BpS	477
CoA	317
CoC	253
CoR	335
CoS	1014
Dis	102
Ep	376
EAs	207
LuC	102
LuS	94
MEN	321
MES	136
Mor	1351
PrN	544
PrS	161
RAm	533
RUS	898
RfE	327
UBr	744
BCh	290
Hat	703
HES	604
HEM	352
HSP	om
H&L	om
LWB	321
RSS	690
RLD	852

CHRISTMAS. C. M.
From GEO. FRED. HANDEL, 1759.

1 Awake, my soul, stretch every nerve,
   And press with vigor on:
   A heavenly race demands thy zeal,
   And an immortal crown.

2 A cloud of witnesses around
   Hold thee in full survey:
   Forget the steps already trod,
   And onward urge thy way.

3 'Tis God's all-animating voice,
   That calls thee from on high;
   'Tis His own hand presents the prize
   To thine aspiring eye:

4 That prize with peerless glories bright,
   Which shall new lustre boast
   When victors' wreaths and monarch's gems
   Shall blend in common dust.

5 Blest Saviour, introduced by Thee,
   Have I my race begun:
   And, crowned with victory, at Thy feet
   I'll lay my honors down.

Rev. Philip Doddridge, 1755.

BpC	741
BpN	416
BpS	955
CoA	397
CoC	625
CoR	480
CoS	880
Dis	42
Ep	476
EAs	547
LuC	458
LuS	450
MEN	594
MES	435
Mor	193
PrN	517
PrS	97
RAm	561
RUS	470
RfE	470
UBr	753
BCh	412
Hat	841
HES	648
HEM	431
HSP	om
H&L	380
LWB	334
RSS	539
RLD	705

CARLISLE. S. M. CHARLES LOCKHART, cir. 1790.

1 Ye servants of the Lord,
  Each in his office wait,
Observant of His heavenly word,
  And watchful at His gate.

2 Let all our lamps be bright,
  And trim the golden flame:
Gird up your loins as in His sight,
  For awful is His name.

3 Watch! 'tis your Lord's command;
  And while we speak, He's near;
Mark the first signal of His hand,
  And ready all appear.

4 Oh, happy servant he
  In such a posture found!
He shall his Lord with rapture see,
  And be with honor crowned.

Rev. Philip Doddridge, 1755.

BpC 732
BpN 453
BpS 927
CoA 250
CoC 618
CoR om
CoS 1060
Dis 107
ED 171
EAs 644
LuC 405
LuS 449
MEN om
MES 460
Mor 1314
PrN 275
PrS om
RAm 664
RUS 554
RfE om
UBr 739

BCh 492
Hat 1141
HES 854
HEM 536
HSP om
H&L 310
LWB om
RSS om
RLD om

DONCASTER. L. M. Arr. EDWARD MILLER, cir. 1790.

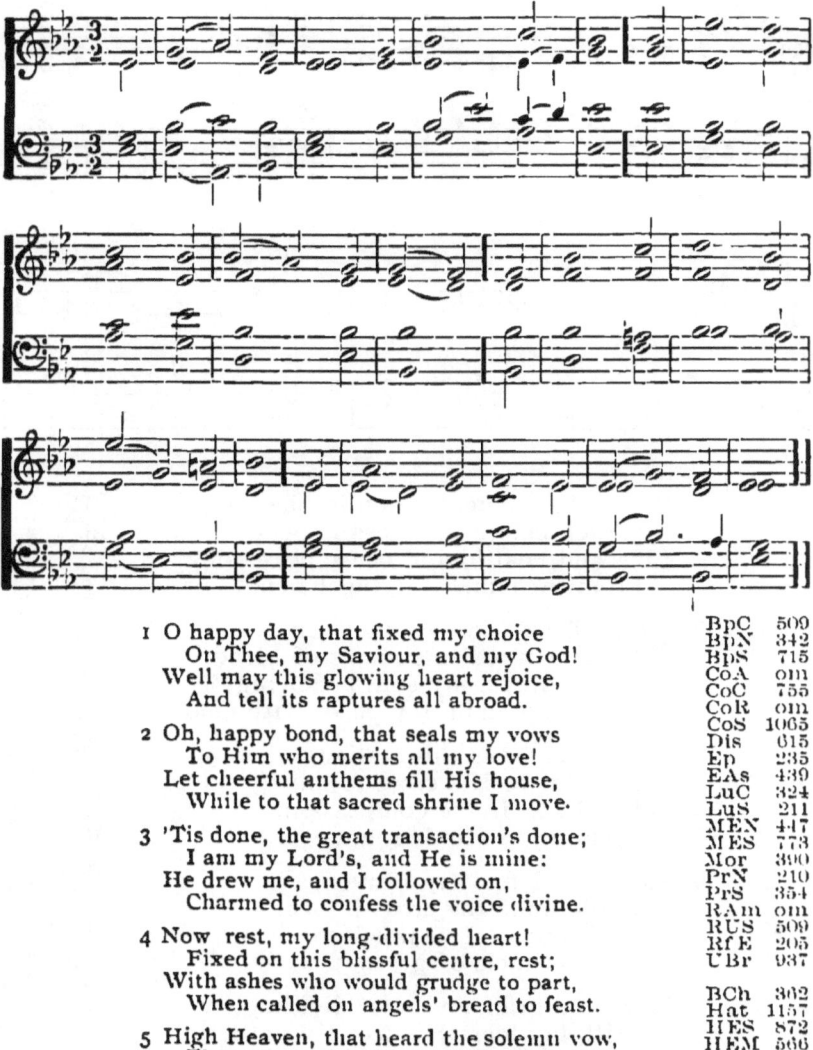

1 O happy day, that fixed my choice
   On Thee, my Saviour, and my God!
   Well may this glowing heart rejoice,
   And tell its raptures all abroad.

2 Oh, happy bond, that seals my vows
   To Him who merits all my love!
   Let cheerful anthems fill His house,
   While to that sacred shrine I move.

3 'Tis done, the great transaction's done;
   I am my Lord's, and He is mine:
   He drew me, and I followed on,
   Charmed to confess the voice divine.

4 Now rest, my long-divided heart!
   Fixed on this blissful centre, rest;
   With ashes who would grudge to part,
   When called on angels' bread to feast.

5 High Heaven, that heard the solemn vow,
   That vow renewed shall daily hear;
   Till in life's latest hour I bow,
   And bless in death a bond so dear.

Rev. Philip Doddridge, 1755.

BpC 509
BpN 342
BpS 715
CoA om
CoC 755
CoR om
CoS 1065
Dis 615
Ep 235
EAs 439
LuC 324
LuS 211
MEN 447
MES 773
Mor 390
PrN 210
PrS 354
RAm om
RUS 509
RfE 205
UBr 937

BCh 362
Hat 1157
HES 872
HEM 566
HSP 705
H&L 446
LWB 258
RSS 857
RLD om

DORRNANCE. 8s & 7s. I. B. WOODBURY, †1858.

1 Sweet the moments, rich in blessing,
  Which before the cross I spend;
Life, and health, and peace possessing,
  From the sinner's dying Friend.

2 Here I'll rest, forever viewing
  Mercy poured in streams of blood:
Precious drops, my soul bedewing,
  Plead and claim my peace with God.

3 Truly blessèd is this station,
  Low before His cross to lie;
While I see divine compassion
  Beaming in His languid eye.

4 Here it is I find my heaven,
  While upon the cross I gaze;
Love I much? I've much forgiven;
  I'm a miracle of grace.

5 Love and grief my heart dividing,
  With my tears His feet I'll bathe;
Constant still, in faith abiding,
  Life deriving from His death.

James Allen, 1757.
Rev. Walter Shirley, 1770.

BpC 257
BpN 353
BpS 487
CoA 104
CoC 536
CoR 533
CoS 295
Dis 501
Ep 84
EAs 319
LuC om
LuS 394
MEN 730
MES 370
Mor 252
PrN 688
PrS 353
RAm 243
RUS 237
RfE 83
UBr 980

BCh 367
Hat 646
HES om
HEM 581
HSP 831
H&L 442
LWB 200
RSS 869
RLD 1026

NETTLETON. 8s & 7s.
Dr. ASAHEL NETTLETON, 1825.

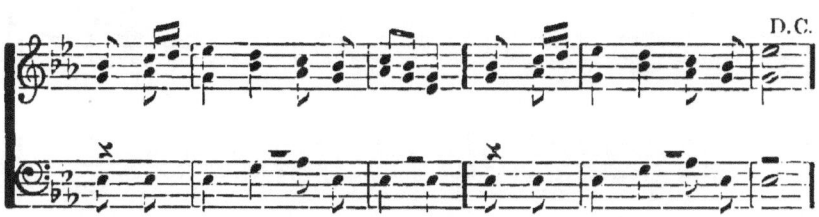

1 Come, Thou fount of every blessing,
   Tune my heart to sing Thy grace;
Streams of mercy, never ceasing,
   Call for songs of loudest praise;
Teach me some melodious sonnet
   Sung by flaming tongues above;
Praise the Mount—I'm fixed upon it!—
   Mount of God's redeeming love.

2 Here I raise my Ebenezer;
   Hither by Thy help I'm come:
And I hope, by Thy good pleasure,
   Safely to arrive at home.
Jesus sought me when a stranger
   Wandering from the fold of God;
He, to rescue me from danger,
   Interposed His precious blood.

3 Oh, to grace how great a debtor
   Daily I'm constrained to be!
Let that grace, now, like a fetter,
   Bind my wandering heart to Thee;
Prone to wander, Lord, I feel it;
   Prone to leave the God I love;
Here's my heart; oh, take and seal it;
   Seal it for Thy courts above.

Rev. Robert Robinson, 1758.

BpC	649
BpN	177
BpS	849
CoA	394
CoC	507
CoR	357
CoS	648
Dis	om
Ep	385
EAs	426
LuC	30
LuS	16
MEN	726
MES	485
Mor	961
PrN	94
PrS	117
RAm	176
RUS	681
RfE	om
UBr	617
BCh	371
Hat	710
HES	536
HEM	350
HSP	850
H&L	315
LWB	om
RSS	818
RLD	1029

HAYDN. S. M.

F. J. HAYDN, 1800.

1 Come, Holy Spirit, come,
    Let Thy bright beams arise;
  Dispel the darkness of our minds,
    And open all our eyes.

2 Revive our drooping faith,
    Our doubts and fears remove,
  And kindle in our breasts the flame
    Of never-dying love.

3 Convince us of our sin,
    Then lead to Jesus' blood,
  And to our wondering view reveal
    The secret love of God.

4 Show us that loving Man,
    That rules the courts of bliss,
  The Lord of hosts, the mighty God,
    The eternal Prince of Peace.

5 'Tis Thine to cleanse the heart,
    To sanctify the soul,
  To pour fresh life in every part,
    And new-create the whole.

6 Dwell therefore in our hearts,
    Our minds from bondage free;
  Then shall we know, and praise, and love
    The Father, Son, and Thee.

Rev. Joseph Hart, 1759.

BpC	373
BpN	206
BpS	538
CoA	189
CoC	234
CoR	147
CoS	452
Dis	om
Ep	135
EAs	164
LuC	254
LuS	324
MEN	om
MES	149
Mor	1329
PrN	879
PrS	130
RAm	365
RUS	321
RfE	134
UBr	378
BCh	181
Hat	334
HES	352
HEM	275
HSP	611
H&L	266
LWB	243
RSS	361
RLD	528

ELIZABETHTOWN. C. M.   GEORGE KINGSLEY, 1838.

1 How oft, alas! this wretched heart
   Has wandered from the Lord!
 How oft my roving thoughts depart,
   Forgetful of His word!

2 Yet sovereign mercy calls—"Return!"
   Dear Lord, and may I come?
 My vile ingratitude I mourn:
   Oh, take the wanderer home!

3 And canst Thou,—wilt Thou yet forgive,
   And bid my crimes remove?
 And shall a pardoned rebel live,
   To speak Thy wondrous love?

4 Almighty grace, Thy healing power,
   How glorious, how divine!
 That can to life and bliss restore
   So vile a heart as mine.

5 Thy pardoning love, so free, so sweet,
   Dear Saviour, I adore;
 Oh, keep me at Thy sacred feet,
   And let me rove no more!

                    Miss Anne Steele, 1760.

BpC	581
BpN	419
BpS	om
CoA	om
CoC	344
CoR	om
CoS	630
Dis	282
Ep	56
EAs	583
LuC	om
LuS	420
MEN	554
MES	om
Mor	om
PrN	404
PrS	210
RAm	om
RUS	156
RfE	58
UBr	629
BCh	325
Hat	620
HES	690
HEM	om
HSP	om
H&L	om
LWB	om
RSS	om
RLD	om

AUTUMN. 8s & 7s. Double.
Spanish Melody.

8s & 7s. Double.

1 Hail, Thou once despisèd Jesus!
    Hail, Thou Galilean King!
  Thou didst suffer to release us,
    Thou didst free salvation bring.
  Hail, Thou agonizing Saviour,
    Bearer of our sin and shame!
  By Thy merits we find favour;
    Life is given through Thy name.

2 Paschal Lamb! by God appointed,
    All our sins on Thee were laid:
  By Almighty love anointed,
    Thou hast full atonement made.
  All Thy people are forgiven
    Through the virtue of Thy blood;
  Opened is the gate of heaven;
    Peace is made 'twixt man and God.

3 Jesus, hail! enthroned in glory,
    There for ever to abide;
  All the heavenly hosts adore Thee,
    Seated at Thy Father's side.
  There for sinners Thou art pleading,
    There Thou dost our place prepare;
  Ever for us interceding,
    Till in glory we appear.

4 Worship, honour, power, and blessing
    Thou art worthy to receive;
  Loudest praises, without ceasing,
    Meet it is for us to give.
  Help, ye bright angelic spirits;
    Bring your sweetest, noblest lays;
  Help to sing our Saviour's merits,
    Help to chant Emmanuel's praise.

                    Rev. John Bakewell, 1757.

BpC	om
BpN	107
BpS	393
CoA	146
CoC	om
CoR	213
CoS	371
Dis	507
Ep	76
EAs	125
LuC	170
LuS	150
MEN	246
MES	103
Mor	955
PrN	172
PrS	82
RAm	331
RUS	308
RfE	98
UBr	355
BCh	122
Hat	434
HES	310
HEM	252
HSP	1307
H&L	149
LWB	om
RSS	282
RLD	422

CHIMES. C. M. LOWELL MASON, 1840.

1 Father of mercies, in Thy word
  What endless glory shines!
  Forever be Thy name adored
  For these celestial lines.

2 Here the Redeemer's welcome voice
  Spreads heavenly peace around;
  And life and everlasting joys
  Attend the blissful sound.

3 Oh may these heavenly pages be
  My ever dear delight;
  And still new beauties may I see,
  And still increasing light.

4 Divine Instructor, gracious Lord,
  Be Thou forever near;
  Teach me to love Thy sacred word,
  And view my Saviour there.

Miss Anne Steele, 1760.

BpC 402
BpN 804
BpS 1156
CoA om
CoC 98
CoR om
CoS 485
Dis om
Ep 362
EAs 176
LuC 310
LuS 249
MEN 299
MES 630
Mor 182
PrN 531
PrS 149
RAm 83
RUS om
RfE 302
UBr 150

BCh 203
Hat 358
HES 396
HEM om
HSP 350
H&L 64
LWB om
RSS 172
RLD 239

NAOMI. C. M.   LOWELL MASON, 1836.

1 Father, whate'er of earthly bliss
   Thy sovereign will denies,
  Accepted at Thy throne of grace
   Let this petition rise:

2 Give me a calm, a thankful heart,
   From every murmur free;
  The blessings of Thy grace impart,
   And make me live to Thee.

3 Let the sweet hope that Thou art mine
   My life and death attend;
  Thy presence through my journey shine
   And crown my journey's end.

Miss Anne Steele, 1760.

BpC 643
BpN 874
BpS 997
CoA 433
CoC 592
CoR 424
CoS 926
Dis 339
Ep 440
EAs 500
LuC 395
LuS 844
MEN 610
MES om
Mor 120
PrN 423
PrS 316
RAm 674
RUS 404
RfE 417
UBr 841

BCh 451
Hat 1026
HES 761
HEM 463
HSP 395
H&L 387
LWB 372
RSS 649
RLD 818

LEONI. 6s, 6s, 8s & 4s. 81.

Hebrew air. Ad. by LEONI, 1770.

6s, 6s, 8s & 4s. 81.

1 The God of Abrah'm praise,
  Who reigns enthroned above:
 Ancient of everlasting days,
  And God of love:
 Jehovah, great I AM!
  By earth and heaven confessed:
 I bow and bless the sacred name,
  For ever blest.

2 The God of Abrah'm praise,
  At whose supreme command
 From earth I rise, and seek the joys
  At His right hand:
 I all on earth forsake,
  Its wisdom, fame, and power;
 And Him my only portion make,
  My shield and tower.

3 He by Himself hath sworn;
  I on His oath depend;
 I shall on eagles' wings upborne
  To heaven ascend:
 I shall behold His face,
  I shall His power adore,
 And sing the wonders of His grace
  For evermore.

4 There dwells the Lord, our King,
  The Lord our righteousness:
 Triumphant o'er the world and sin,
  The Prince of Peace,
 On Zion's sacred height,
  His kingdom still maintains,
 And glorious, with His saints in light,
  For ever reigns.

5 The whole triumphant host
  Give thanks to God on high:
 "Hail, Father, Son, and Holy Ghost!"
  They ever cry.
 Hail, Abrah'm's God and mine!
  (I join the heavenly lays)
 All might and majesty are Thine,
  And endless praise!

Rev. Thomas Oliver, 1770.

```
BpC   122
BpN   om
BpS   1292
CoA   11
CoC   om
CoR   om
CoS   116
Dis   om
Ep    141
EAs   om
LuC   381
LuS   om
MEN   1075
MES   423
Mor   1192
PrN   om
PrS   432
RAm   107
RUS   om
RfE   140
UBr   om

BCh   9
Hat   264
HES   1386
HEM   714
HSP   1264
H&L   om
LWB   111
RSS   95
RLD   153
```

FEDERAL STREET. L. M.
HENRY K. OLIVER, 1832.

1. Jesus! and shall it ever be,
   A mortal man ashamed of Thee?
   Ashamed of Thee, whom angels praise,
   Whose glories shine through endless days?

2. Ashamed of Jesus! just as soon
   Let midnight be ashamed of noon;
   'Tis midnight with my soul till He,
   Bright morning star, bids darkness flee.

3. Ashamed of Jesus! sooner far
   Let evening blush to own a star:
   He sheds the beams of light divine
   O'er this benighted soul of mine.

4. Ashamed of Jesus! that dear Friend
   On Whom my hopes of heaven depend!
   No; when I blush, be this my shame,
   That I no more revere His name.

5. Ashamed of Jesus! yes, I may,
   When I've no guilt to wash away,
   No tear to wipe, no good to crave,
   No fear to quell, no soul to save.

6. Till then, nor is my boasting vain,
   Till then I boast a Saviour slain;
   And oh may this my glory be,
   That Christ is not ashamed of me.

Rev. Joseph Grigg, 1765.
Rev. Benjamin Francis, 1787.

BpC	738
BpN	446
BpS	712
CoA	230
CoC	542
CoR	375
CoS	798
Dis	131
Ep	218
EAs	440
LuC	445
LuS	174
MEN	604
MES	472
Mor	377
PrN	602
PrS	356
RAm	559
RUS	188
RfE	207
UBr	om
BCh	164
Hat	764
HES	616
HEM	439
HSP	62
H&L	om
LWB	345
RSS	597
ELD	805

OLIPHANT. 8s, 7s & 4s.
LOWELL MASON, 1832.

1 Guide me, O Thou great Jehovah,
   Pilgrim through this barren land·
I am weak, but Thou art mighty,
   Hold me with Thy powerful hand.
     Bread of heaven,
   Feed me till I want no more.

2 Open now the crystal fountain,
   Whence the healing streams do flow:
Let the fiery cloudy pillar
   Lead me all my journey through;
     Strong deliverer!
   Be Thou still my strength and shield.

3 When I tread the verge of Jordan,
   Bid my anxious fears subside:
Death of death and hell's destruction,
   Land me safe on Canaan's side;
     Songs of praises
   I will ever give to Thee.

Rev. Peter Williams, 1771.
Rev. William Williams, 1773.

BpC	971
BpN	99
BpS	1029
CoA	432
CoC	606
CoR	564
CoS	1221
Dis	519
Ep	505
EAs	81
LuC	418
LuS	387
MEN	171
MES	427
Mor	1381
PrN	473
PrS	57
RAm	691
RUS	200
Rf E	321
UBr	807
BCh	464
Hat	913
HES	662
HEM	399
HSP	825
H&L	346
LWB	135
RNS	134
RLD	745

ZION. 8s, 7s & 4s. THOMAS HASTINGS, 1830.

1 O'er the gloomy hills of darkness
   Look, my soul! be still,—and gaze;
  See the promises advancing
   To a glorious day of grace:
    Blessèd jubilee!
   Let Thy glorious morning dawn.

2 Let the dark, benighted pagan,
   Let the rude barbarian see
  That divine and glorious conquest,
   Once obtained on Calvary:
    Let the gospel
   Loud resound, from pole to pole!

3 Kingdoms wide that sit in darkness—
   Grant them, Lord, the glorious light;
  Now from eastern coast to western
   May the morning chase the night;
    Let redemption,
   Freely purchased, win the day.

4 Fly abroad, thou mighty gospel!
   Win and conquer,—never cease;
  May Thy lasting, wide dominions
   Multiply and still increase:
    Sway Thy scepter,
   Saviour! all the world around.

Rev. William Williams, 1772.

BpC 903
BpN 607
BpS 1220
CoA 281
CoC 876
CoR om
CoS 1127
Dis 530
Ep 288
EAs om
LuC 296
LuS om
MEN 940
MES 621
Mor 1404
PrN 650
PrS 597
RAm 820
RUS 140
RfE om
UBr 1052

BCh 580
Hat 1247
HES 1081
HEM 640
HSP om
H&L om
LWB om
RSS 901
RLD 1069

NUREMBURG. 7s.   JOH. RUD. AHLE, 1664.

1 Praise to God, immortal praise,
  For the love that crowns our days!
  Bounteous source of every joy,
  Let Thy praise our tongues employ!

2 For the blessings of the field,
  For the stores the gardens yield,
  For the vine's exalted juice,
  For the generous olive's use;

3 Flocks that whiten all the plain;
  Yellow sheaves of ripened grain:
  Clouds that drop their fattening dews;
  Suns that temperate warmth diffuse;

4 All that Spring, with bounteous hand,
  Scatters o'er the smiling land;
  All that liberal Autumn pours
  From her overflowing stores;

5 These, great God, to Thee we owe,
  Source whence all our blessings flow;
  And, for these, our souls shall raise
  Grateful vows, and solemn praise.

              Mrs. Anna Laetitia Barbauld, 1772.

BpC	946
BpN	688
BpS	249
CoA	583
CoC	928
CoR	651
CoS	1142
Dis	125
Ep	302
EAs	779
LuC	501
LuS	549
MEN	1084
MES	om
Mor	43
PrN	829
PrS	om
RAm	896
RUS	617
RfE	230
UBr	1223
BCh	549
Hat	1291
HES	1154
HEM	731
HSP	om
H&L	531
LWB	130
RSS	1050
RLD	1151

GREENVILLE. 8s & 7s. Double.
J. J. ROUSSEAU, 1750.

1 Lord, dismiss us with Thy blessing,
   Fill our hearts with joy and peace;
Let us each, Thy love possessing,
   Triumph in redeeming grace:
      O refresh us,
Travelling through this wilderness.

2 Thanks we give and adoration
   For Thy gospel's joyful sound;
May the fruits of Thy salvation
   In our hearts and lives abound;
      May Thy presence
With us evermore be found.

3 So, whene'er the signal's given,
   Us from earth to call away,
Borne on angels' wings to heaven,
   Glad the summons to obey,
      May we ever
Reign with Christ in endless day.

Rev. John Fawcett, 1773.

BpC	47
BpN	20
BpS	86
CoA	549
CoC	78
CoR	35
CoS	86
Dis	521
Ep	165
EAs	38
LuC	58
LuS	594
MEN	52
MES	om
Mor	1395
PrN	86
PrS	486
RAm	73
RUS	680
RfE	541
UBr	141
BCh	240
Hat	84
HES	963
HEM	19
HSP	829
H&L	om
LWB	496
RSS	136
RLD	206

BOYLSTON. S. M.
LOWELL MASON, 1832.

1 Blest be the tie that binds
　Our hearts in Christian love:
　The fellowship of kindred minds
　　Is like to that above.

2 Before our Father's throne
　We pour our ardent prayers;
　Our fears, our hopes, our aims are one,
　　Our comforts and our cares.

3 We share our mutual woes,
　Our mutual burdens bear;
　And often for each other flows
　　The sympathizing tear.

4 When we asunder part,
　It gives us inward pain;
　But we shall still be joined in heart,
　　And hope to meet again.

5 This glorious hope revives
　Our courage by the way;
　While each in expectation lives,
　　And longs to see the day.

6 From sorrow, toil, and pain,
　And sin, we shall be free,
　And perfect love and friendship reign
　　Through all eternity.

　　　　Rev. John Fawcett, 1782.

BpC 755
BpN 463
BpS 779
CoA 301
CoC 661
CoR 497
CoS 857
Dis 408
Ep 315
EAs 632
LuC om
LuS 434
MEN 797
MES 716
Mor 1335
PrN 597
PrS 298
RAm 770
RUS 360
RfE 160
UBr 992

BCh 402
Hat 1177
HES 925
HEM 597
HSP 544
H&L om
LWB 421
RSS 824
RLD 941

TOPLADY. S. M.   THOMAS HASTINGS, 1830.

1. Rock of Ages! cleft for me,
   Let me hide myself in Thee!
   Let the water and the blood,
   From Thy riven side that flowed,
   Be of sin the double cure—
   Cleanse me from its guilt and power.

2. Not the labor of my hands
   Can fulfil Thy law's demands;
   Could my zeal no respite know,
   Could my tears for ever flow—
   All for sin could not atone:
   Thou must save, and Thou alone!

3. Nothing in my hand I bring;
   Simply to Thy cross I cling,
   Naked, come to Thee for dress;
   Helpless, look to Thee for grace;
   Foul, I to the fountain fly;
   Wash me, Saviour, or I die!

4. While I draw this fleeting breath,
   When my eyelids close in death,
   When I soar to worlds unknown,
   See Thee on Thy judgment throne,—
   Rock of Ages! cleft for me,
   Let me hide myself in Thee!

         Rev. Augustus Toplady, 1776.

BpC	258
BpN	496
BpS	692
CoA	350
CoC	552
CoR	298
CoS	721
Dis	474
Ep	301
EAs	281
LuC	367
LuS	310
MEN	415
MES	88
Mor	1280
PrN	301
PrS	47
RAm	406
RUS	208
RfE	880
UBr	515
BCh	140
Hat	697
HES	499
HEM	332
HSP	1124
H&L	169
LWB	195
RSS	874
RLD	962

84

SOLITUDE. 7s.

L. T. DOWNES, 1851.

1 Hark, my soul! it is the Lord;
  'Tis thy Saviour—hear His word;
  Jesus speaks, and speaks to thee:
  "Say, poor sinner, lovest thou me?

2 "I delivered thee when bound,
  And, when bleeding, healed thy wound:
  Sought thee wandering, set thee right,
  Turned thy darkness into light.

3 "Can a woman's tender care
  Cease toward the child she bare?
  Yes, she may forgetful be,
  Yet will I remember thee.

4 "Mine is an unchanging love,
  Higher than the heights above;
  Deeper than the depths beneath—
  Free and faithful—strong as death.

5 "Thou shalt see My glory soon,
  When the work of grace is done;
  Partner of My throne shalt be!
  Say, poor sinner! lovest thou me?"

6 Lord! it is my chief complaint
  That my love is weak and faint;
  Yet I love Thee, and adore;—
  Oh for grace to love Thee more.

BpC 530
BpN 335
BpS 728
CoA 336
CoC 577
CoR 314
CoS 709
Dis om
Ep 521
EAs om
LuC om
LuS 451
MEN 552
MES 366
Mor 59
PrN 288
PrS 42
RAm 718
RUS 541
RfE 424
UBr 576

BCh 159
Hat 790
HES 881
HEM 498
HSP 1425
H&L 275
LWB om
RSS 830
RLD 1007

William Cowper, 1768.

COWPER. C. M.   LOWELL MASON, 1830.

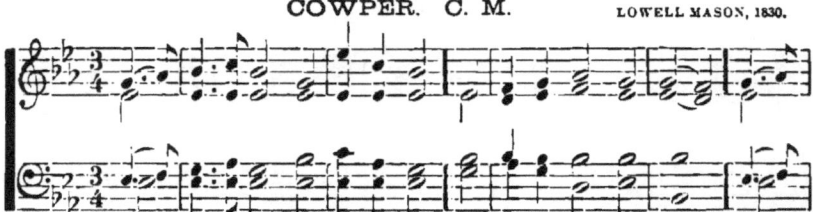

1 There is a fountain filled with blood,
   Drawn from Immanuel's veins;
And sinners, plunged beneath that flood,
   Lose all their guilty stains.

2 The dying thief rejoiced to see
   That fountain in his day;
And there have I, as vile as he,
   Washed all my sins away.

3 Dear, dying Lamb! Thy precious blood
   Shall never lose its power,
Till all the ransomed church of God
   Be saved, to sin no more.

4 E'er since, by faith, I saw the stream
   Thy flowing wounds supply,
Redeeming love has been my theme,
   And shall be till I die.

5 Then, in a nobler, sweeter song,
   I'll sing Thy power to save,
When this poor, lisping, stammering tongue
   Lies silent in the grave.

William Cowper, 1772.

BpC	414
BpN	231
BpS	473
CoA	103
CoC	264
CoR	190
CoS	300
Dis	623
Ep	383
EAs	192
LuC	159
LuS	136
MEN	319
MES	86
Mor	92
PrN	136
PrS	165
RAm	410
RUS	210
RfE	331
UBr	411
BCh	279
Hat	450
HES	501
HEM	334
HSP	652
H&L	286
LWB	198
RSS	398
RLD	568

BALERMA. C. M.
Spanish Melody.

1 Oh for a closer walk with God,
   A calm and heavenly frame,—
A light to shine upon the road
   That leads me to the Lamb!

2 Where is the blessedness I knew,
   When first I saw the Lord?
Where is the soul-refreshing view
   Of Jesus and His word?

3 What peaceful hours I once enjoyed!
   How sweet their memory still!
But they have left an aching void
   The world can never fill.

4 Return, O holy Dove! return,
   Sweet messenger of rest!
I hate the sins that made Thee mourn,
   And drove Thee from my breast:

5 The dearest idol I have known,
   Whate'er that idol be,
Help me to tear it from Thy throne,
   And worship only Thee.

6 So shall my walk be close with God,
   Calm and serene my frame;
So purer light shall mark the road
   That leads me to the Lamb.

William Cowper, 1772.

BpC	592
BpN	375
BpS	942
CoA	476
CoC	449
CoR	om
CoS	627
Dis	347
Ep	435
EAs	582
LuC	396
LuS	392
MEN	549
MES	341
Mor	om
PrN	426
PrS	317
RAm	597
RUS	157
RfE	459
UBr	625
BCh	418
Hat	945
HES	684
HEM	487
HSP	490
H&L	389
LWB	357
RSS	493
RLD	667

DOWNS. C. M.

LOWELL MASON, 1832.

1 God moves in a mysterious way
  His wonders to perform;
He plants His footsteps in the sea,
  And rides upon the storm.

2 Deep in unfathomable mines
  Of never-failing skill,
He treasures up His bright designs,
  And works His sovereign will.

3 Ye fearful saints, fresh courage take;
  The clouds ye so much dread
Are big with mercy, and shall break
  In blessings on your head.

4 Judge not the Lord by feeble sense,
  But trust Him for His grace;
Behind a frowning providence
  He hides a smiling face.

5 His purposes will ripen fast,
  Unfolding ev'ry hour;
The bud may have a bitter taste,
  But sweet will be the flower.

6 Blind unbelief is sure to err,
  And scan His work in vain;
God is His own interpreter,
  And He will make it plain.

William Cowper, 1774.

BpC	160
BpN	81
BpS	193
CoA	454
CoC	153
CoR	111
CoS	236
Dis	36
Ep	502
EAs	69
LuC	82
LuS	76
MEN	161
MES	16
Mor	89
PrN	369
PrS	26
RAm	131
RUS	47
RfE	317
UBr	848
BCh	57
Hat	1043
HES	116
HEM	466
HSP	643
H&L	91
LWB	om
RSS	209
RLD	280

HEBER. C. M.   GEORGE KINGSLEY, 1838.

1 Approach, my soul, the mercy-seat
  Where Jesus answers prayer;
There humbly fall before His feet,
  For none can perish there.

2 Thy promise is my only plea,
  With this I venture nigh;
Thou callest burdened souls to Thee,
  And such, O Lord, am I.

3 Bowed down beneath a load of sin,
  By Satan sorely pressed;
By war without and fears within,
  I come to Thee for rest.

4 Be Thou my shield and hiding-place,
  That, sheltered near Thy side,
I may my fierce accuser face,
  And tell him Thou hast died.

5 O wondrous love! to bleed and die,
  To bear the cross and shame,
That guilty sinners, such as I,
  Might plead Thy gracious name.

6 Poor tempest-tossèd soul, be still,
  My promised grace receive;"
'Tis Jesus speaks;—I must, I will,
  I can, I do believe.

Rev. John Newton, 1779.

BpC	579
BpN	290
BpS	663
CoA	355
CoC	687
CoR	404
CoS	om
Dis	354
Ep	399
EAs	264
LuC	364
LuS	330
MEN	om
MES	327
Mor	164
PrN	64
PrS	379
RAm	673
RUS	732
RtE	363
UBr	482
BCh	392
Hat	622
HES	455
HEM	320
HSP	om
H&L	337
LWB	261
RSS	515
RLD	104

HORTON. 7s. X. S. Von WARTENSEE, 1786.

1 Come, my soul, thy suit prepare;
  Jesus loves to answer prayer;
  He Himself has bid thee pray,
  Therefore will not say thee nay.

2 Thou art coming to a King;
  Large petitions with thee bring,
  For His grace and power are such,
  None can ever ask too much.

3 With my burden I begin;
  Lord, remove this load of sin!
  Let Thy blood, for sinners spilt,
  Set my conscience free from guilt.

4 Lord, I come to Thee for rest;
  Take possession of my breast;
  There Thy blood-bought right maintain,
  And without a rival reign.

5 While I am a pilgrim here,
  Let Thy love my spirit cheer;
  As my Guide, my Guard, my Friend,
  Lead me to my journey's end.

6 Show me what I have to do,
  Every hour my strength renew;
  Let me live a life of faith;
  Let me die Thy people's death.

  Rev. John Newton, 1779.

BpC 621
BpN 403
BpS 6
CoA 472
CoC 701
CoR 396
CoS om
Dis om
Ep 401
EAs 431
LuC 29
LuS om
MEN 718
MES 312
Mor 72
PrN 60
PrS 470
RAm 39
RUS om
RfE 383
UBr 804

BCh 390
Hat 916
HES 979
HEM 24
HSP om
H&L 332
LWB om
RSS 61
RLD 108

BENEVENTO. 7s. Double.   SAMUEL WEBBE, 1770.

1 While with ceaseless course the sun
   Hasted through the former year,
 Many souls their race have run,
   Never more to meet us here:
 Fixed in an eternal state,
   They have done with all below;
 We a little longer wait,
   But how little, none can know.

2 As the wingèd arrow flies
   Speedily the mark to find,—
 As the lightning from the skies
   Darts, and leaves no trace behind,—
 Swiftly thus our fleeting days
   Bear us down life's rapid stream:
 Upward, Lord, our spirits raise!
   All below is but a dream.

3 Thanks for mercies past receive;
   Pardon of our sins renew;
 Teach us henceforth how to live
   With eternity in view;
 Bless Thy word to young and old;
   Fill us with a Saviour's love;
 When our life's short tale is told,
   May we dwell with Thee above.

                Rev. John Newton, 1774.

```
BpC   961
BpN   702
BpS  1294
CoA   600
CoC   916
CoR   640
CoS  1248
Dis   om
Ep     31
EAs   785
LuC   139
LuS   544
MEN   956
MES   658
Mor  1073
PrN   807
PrS   508
RAm   882
RUS   om
RtE    32
UBr   om

BCh   558
Hat  1333
HES  1261
HEM   727
HSP   om
H&L   541
LWB   522
RSS  1048
RLD    11
```

SABBATH. 7s. 61. LOWELL MASON, 1834.

1 Safely through another week
    God has brought us on our way;
  Let us now a blessing seek,
    Waiting in His courts to-day:
  Day of all the week the best,
  Emblem of eternal rest.

2 While we pray for pardoning grace,
    Through the dear Redeemer's name,
  Show Thy reconciled face;
    Take away our sin and shame:
  From our worldly cares set free,
  May we rest this day in Thee.

3 Here we come, Thy name to praise;
    Let us feel Thy presence near;
  May Thy glory meet our eyes,
    While we in Thy house appear:
  Here afford us, Lord, a taste
  Of our everlasting feast.

4 May Thy gospel's joyful sound
    Conquer sinners, comfort saints;
  Make the fruits of grace abound;
    Bring relief for all complaints:
  Thus let all our Sabbaths prove,
  Till we join the church above.

Rev. John Newton, 1774.

BpC 63
BpN 36
BpS 2
CoA 537
CoC 9
CoR 3
CoS 55
Dis 132
Ep 350
EAs om
LuC 37
LuS 36
MEN 88
MES 233
Mor 1284
PrN 83
PrS 460
RAm 5
RUS 637
RfE 153
UBr 94

BCh 210
Hat 37
HES 953
HEM 67
HSP 1062
H&L om
LWB 440
RSS 13
RLD 81

ST. PETER. C. M.
A. R. REINAGLE, 1840.

1 How sweet the name of Jesus sounds
   In a believer's ear!
It soothes his sorrows, heals his wounds,
   And drives away his fear.

2 It makes the wounded spirit whole,
   And calms the troubled breast;
'Tis manna to the hungry soul,
   And to the weary rest.

3 Dear name! the rock on which I build,
   My shield and hiding-place,
My never-failing treasury, filled
   With boundless stores of grace.

4 Jesus! my Shepherd, Guardian, Friend,
   My Prophet, Priest, and King,
My Lord, my Life, my Way, my End,
   Accept the praise I bring.

5 Weak is the effort of my heart,
   And cold my warmest thought;
But when I see Thee as Thou art,
   I'll praise Thee as I ought.

6 Till then I would Thy love proclaim
   With ev'ry fleeting breath;
And may the music of Thy name
   Refresh my soul in death.

Rev. John Newton 1779.

BpC	327
BpN	170
BpS	470
CoA	497
CoC	510
CoR	232
CoS	441
Dis	318
Ep	395
EAs	94
LuC	221
LuS	175
MEN	316
MES	138
Mor	130
PrN	229
PrS	296
RAm	517
RUS	674
RfE	427
UBr	538
BCh	160
Hat	746
HES	504
HEM	371
HSP	384
H&L	133
LWB	144
RSS	613
RLD	772

AUSTRIA. 8s, 7s. D.

F. J. HAYDN, 1797.

8s, 7s. Double.

1 Glorious things of thee are spoken,
    Zion, city of our God!
He, whose word cannot be broken,
    Formed thee for His own abode:
On the Rock of Ages founded,
    What can shake thy sure repose?
With salvation's walls surrounded,
    Thou mayst smile at all thy foes.

2 See! the streams of living waters,
    Springing from eternal love,
Well supply thy sons and daughters,
    And all fear of want remove:
Who can faint while such a river
    Ever flows their thirst t' assuage?
Grace which, like the Lord the giver,
    Never fails from age to age.

3 Round each habitation hovering,
    See the cloud and fire appear,
For a glory and a covering,
    Showing that the Lord is near:
Thus deriving from their banner
    Light by night, and shade by day,
Safe they feed upon the manna,
    Which He gives them when they pray.

4 Saviour, if of Zion's city
    I through grace a member am,
Let the world deride or pity,
    I will glory in Thy name:
Fading is the worldling's pleasure,
    All his boasted pomp and show:
Solid joys and lasting treasure
    None but Zion's children know.

              Rev. John Newton, 1779.

BpC	803
PpN	518
BpS	815
CoA	200
CoC	723
CoR	502
CoS	1023
Dis	504
Ep	190
EAs	615
LuC	266
LuS	193
MEN	776
MES	179
Mor	937
PrN	651
PrS	603
RAm	692
RUS	443
RfE	168
UBr	921
BCh	479
Hat	1116
HES	831
HEM	603
HSP	1072
H&L	527
LWB	446
RSS	753
RLD	944

BREST. 8s, 7s & 4s.
LOWELL MASON, 1836.

1 Day of judgment, day of wonders!
  Hark! the trumpet's awful sound,
Louder than a thousand thunders,
  Shakes the vast creation round:
    How the summons
Will the sinner's heart confound!

2 See the Judge, our nature wearing,
  Clothed in majesty divine:
You who long for His appearing,
  Then shall say, "This God is mine:"
    Glorious Saviour!
Own me in that day for Thine.

3 At His call the dead awaken,
  Rise to life from earth and sea;
All the powers of nature, shaken
  By His voice, prepare to flee:
    Careless sinner,
What will then become of thee?

4 But to those who have confessed,
  Loved and served the Lord below,
He will say, "Come near, ye blessed;
  See the kingdom I bestow:
    You forever
Shall My love and glory know."

Rev. John Newton, 1774.

BpC 1024
BpN 663
BpS 615
CoA om
CoC 882
CoR om
CoS 1287
Dis 533
Ep 481
EAs 844
LuC om
LuS 571
MEN 1029
MES om
Mor 1377
PrN om
PrS 662
RAm om
RUS 15
RfE 485
UBr om

BCh om
Hat 1403
HES 1341
HEM om
HSP om
H&L om
LWB om
RSS 972
RLD 1111

LABAN. S. M.
LOWELL MASON, 1830.

1 My soul, be on thy guard,
    Ten thousand foes arise;
And hosts of sin are pressing hard
    To draw thee from the skies.

2 O watch, and fight, and pray,
    The battle ne'er give o'er;
Renew the conflict every day,
    And help divine implore.

3 Ne'er think the victory won,
    Nor once at ease sit down;
Thy arduous work will not be done
    Till thou obtain thy crown.

4 Fight on, my soul, till death
    Shall bring thee to thy God;
He'll take thee, at thy parting breath,
    Up to His blest abode.
                  George Heath, 1781.

BpC	748
BpN	422
BpS	958
CoA	403
CoC	619
CoR	487
CoS	636
Dis	431
Ep	470
EAs	566
LuC	463
LuS	457
MEN	581
MES	523
Mor	1341
PrN	510
PrS	384
RAm	568
RUS	463
RfE	474
UBr	763
BCh	478
Hat	960
HES	630
HEM	425
HSP	557
H&L	354
LWB	341
RSS	547
RLD	723

CORONATION. C. M.
OLIVER HOLDEN, 1793.

C. M.

1 All hail the power of Jesus' name!
  Let angels prostrate fall;
  Bring forth the royal diadem,
  And crown Him Lord of all!

2 Crown Him, ye morning stars of light,
  Who fixed this floating ball;
  Now hail the Strength of Israel's might,
  And crown Him Lord of all.

3 Crown Him, ye martyrs of our God,
  Who from His altar call!
  Extol the Stem of Jesse's rod,
  And crown Him Lord of all.

4 Ye seed of Israel's chosen race,
  Ye ransomed from the fall,
  Hail Him who saves you by His grace,
  And crown Him Lord of all.

5 Hail Him, ye heirs of David's line,
  Whom David Lord did call;
  The God incarnate, Man divine,
  And crown Him Lord of all.

6 Sinners, whose love can ne'er forget,
  The wormwood and the gall,
  Go, spread your trophies at His feet,
  And crown Him Lord of all.

7 Let every kindred, every tribe,
  On this terrestrial ball,
  To Him all majesty ascribe,
  And crown Him Lord of all.

8 Oh that with yonder sacred throng
  We at His feet may fall;
  We'll join the everlasting song,
  And crown Him Lord of all.

Rev. Edward Perronet, 1780.
Dr. John Rippon, 1787.

BpC	301
BpN	161
BpS	446
CoA	120
CoC	207
CoR	209
CoS	379
Dis	74
Ep	424
EAs	93
LuC	215
LuS	149
MEN	218
MES	105
Mor	162
PrN	32
PrS	119
RAm	320
RUS	277
RfE	394
UBr	336
BCh	120
Hat	516
HES	329
HEM	241
HSP	363
H&L	114
LWB	216
RSS	329
RLD	471

CONSUMMATUM EST. 8s, 7s & 4s.   JOHN STANLEY.

1 Hark! the voice of love and mercy
    Sounds aloud from Calvary;
  See, it rends the rocks asunder,
    Shakes the earth, and veils the sky:
      "It is finished!"
  Hear the dying Saviour cry.

2 "It is finished!"—oh, what pleasure
    Do these precious words afford!
  Heavenly blessings without measure
    Flow to us from Christ the Lord.
      "It is finished!"
  Saints, the dying words record.

3 Finished all the types and shadows
    Of the ceremonial law,—
  Finished—all that God hath promised;
    Death and hell no more shall awe:
      "It is finished!"
  Saints, from hence your comfort draw.

4 Tune your harps anew, ye seraphs,
    Join to sing the pleasing theme;
  All on earth and all in heaven
    Join to praise Immanuel's name:
      Hallelujah!
  Glory to the bleeding Lamb!

                          Rev. Jonathan Evans, 1784.

BpC	252
BpN	132
BpS	358
CoA	105
CoC	210
CoR	om
CoS	297
Dis	om
Ep	88
EAs	127
LuC	om
LuS	138
MEN	224
MES	85
Mor	1399
PrN	140
PrS	81
RAm	272
RUS	238
RfE	93
UBr	302
BCh	om
Hat	436
HES	252
HEM	om
HSP	1304
H&L	228
LWB	om
RSS	315
RLD	390

ARIEL. C. P. M.
LOWELL MASON, 1835.

1 Oh, could I speak the matchless worth,
Oh, could I sound the glories forth
  Which in my Saviour shine!
I'd soar, and touch the heavenly strings,
And vie with Gabriel, while he sings,
  In notes almost divine.

2 I'd sing the precious blood He spilt,
My ransom from the dreadful guilt
  Of sin and wrath divine:
I'd sing His glorious righteousness,
In which all perfect heavenly dress
  My soul shall ever shine.

3 I'd sing the characters He bears,
And all the forms of love He wears,
  Exalted on His throne:
In loftiest songs of sweetest praise,
I would to everlasting days
  Make all His glories known.

4 Well, the delightful day will come
When my dear Lord will bring me home,
  When I shall see His face:
Then with my Saviour, Brother, Friend,
A blest eternity I'll spend,
  Triumphant in His grace.

Rev. Samuel Medley, 1789.

BpC	320
BpN	192
BpS	425
CoA	496
CoC	304
CoR	214
CoS	433
Dis	75
Ep	374
EAs	436
LuC	om
LuS	159
MEN	743
MES	om
Mor	om
PrN	90
PrS	40
RAm	512
RUS	423
RfE	333
UBr	623
BCh	157
Hat	776
HES	588
HEM	386
HSP	868
H&L	124
LWB	154
RSS	616
RLD	418

PORTUGUESE HYMN. 11s.
JOHN READING, 1760.

PORTUGUESE HYMN. 11s. Concluded.

1 How firm a foundation, ye saints of the Lord,
Is laid for your faith in His excellent word!
What more can he say than to you He hath said,
Who unto the Saviour for refuge have fled:—

2 "Fear not, I am with thee; oh, be not dismayed;
For I am thy God, I will still give thee aid:
I'll strengthen thee, help thee, and cause thee to stand,
Upheld by My righteous, omnipotent hand.

3 "When through the deep waters I call thee to go,
The rivers of sorrow shall not overflow;
For I will be with thee thy troubles to bless,
And sanctify to thee thy deepest distress.

4 "When through fiery trials thy pathway shall lie,
My grace, all-sufficient, shall be thy supply;
The flame shall not hurt thee; I only design
Thy dross to consume and thy gold to refine.

5 "Ev'n down to old age all My people shall prove
My sovereign, eternal, unchangeable love;
And then, when gray hairs shall their temples adorn,
Like lambs they shall still in My bosom be borne.

6 "The soul that to Jesus hath fled for repose,
I will not, I will not desert to his foes:
That soul, though all hell should endeavor to shake,
I'll never—no, never—no, never forsake!"

George Keith (?), 1787.

BRATTLE STREET. C. M. Double.
IGNAZ PLEYEL, 1831.

1. While Thee I seek, protecting Power!
   Be my vain wishes stilled;
   And may this consecrated hour
   With better hopes be filled!
   Thy love the powers of thought bestowed;
   To Thee my thoughts would soar:
   Thy mercy o'er my life has flowed;
   That mercy I adore.

2. In each event of life, how clear
   Thy ruling hand I see!
   Each blessing to my soul more dear
   Because conferred by Thee.
   In every joy that crowns my days,
   In every pain I bear,
   My heart shall find delight in praise,
   Or seek relief in prayer.

3. When gladness wings my favored hour,
   Thy love my thoughts shall fill;
   Resigned, when storms of sorrow lower,
   My soul shall meet Thy will.
   My lifted eye, without a tear,
   The gathering storm shall see;
   My steadfast heart shall know no fear;
   That heart will rest on Thee.

Miss Helen Maria Williams, 1790.

BpC	25
BpN	13
BpS	59
CoA	486
CoC	14
CoR	116
CoS	4
Dis	346
Ep	441
EAs	70
LuC	16
LuS	51
MEN	616
MES	772
Mor	1452
PrN	432
PrS	24
RAm	123
RUS	372
RfE	316
UBr	810
BCh	226
Hat	1033
HES	124
HEM	470
HSP	911
H&L	376
LWB	128
RSS	185
RLD	259

104

FAITH. C. M.
Dr. S. P. TUCKERMAN, 1849.

1. O Thou, from whom all goodness flows,
   I lift my soul to Thee;
   In all my sorrows, conflicts, woes,
   O Lord, remember me!

2. When on my aching burdened heart,
   My sins lie heavily,
   Thy pardon grant, new peace impart;
   Thus, Lord, remember me!

3. When trials sore obstruct my way,
   And ills I cannot flee,
   Oh, let my strength be as my day—
   Dear Lord, remember me!

4. When in the solemn hour of death
   I wait Thy just decree;
   Be this the prayer of my last breath:
   Now, Lord, remember me!

5. And when before Thy throne I stand,
   And lift my soul to Thee,
   Then with the saints at Thy right hand,
   O Lord, remember me!

Rev. Thomas Haweis, 1791.
Rev. Thomas Cotterill, 1819.

BpC	687
BpN	om
BpS	994
CoA	437
CoC	447
CoR	281
CoS	939
Dis	om
Ep	65
EAs	414
LuC	490
LuS	378
MEN	619
MES	499
Mor	om
PrN	236
PrS	417
RAm	433
RUS	194
RfE	62
UBr	om
BCh	om
Hat	1040
HES	762
HEM	om
HSP	om
H&L	399
LWB	om
RSS	455
RLD	641

SHIRLAND. S. M.
SAMUEL STANLEY, 1800.

1. I love Thy kingdom, Lord,
   The house of Thine abode,
   The Church our blest Redeemer saved
   With His own precious blood.

2. I love Thy Church, O God;
   Her walls before Thee stand
   Dear as the apple of Thine eye,
   And graven on Thy hand.

3. If e'er to bless her sons
   My voice or hands deny,
   These hands let useful skill forsake,
   This voice in silence die.

4. For her my tears shall fall,
   For her my prayers ascend;
   To her my cares and toils be given,
   Till toils and cares shall end.

5. Beyond my highest joy
   I prize her heavenly ways,
   Her sweet communion, solemn vows,
   Her hymns of love and praise.

6. Jesus, Thou friend divine,
   Our Saviour and our King,
   Thy hand from every snare and foe
   Shall great deliverance bring.

7. Sure as Thy truth shall last,
   To Zion shall be given
   The brightest glories earth can yield
   And brighter bliss of heaven.

Rev. Timothy Dwight, 1800.

BpC	784
BpN	520
BpS	832
CoA	206
CoC	720
CoR	507
CoS	1017
Dis	456
Ep	191
EAs	612
LuC	275
Lus	202
MEN	770
MES	708
Mor	1352
PrN	575
PrS	P137
RAm	693
RUS	406
RfE	170
UBr	914
BCh	485
Hat	1094
HES	835
HEM	599
HSP	om
H&L	394
LWB	91
RSS	35
RLD	918

DRESDEN.

GERMAN.

1 Dread Jehovah! God of nations!
   From Thy temple in the skies,
   Hear Thy people's supplications;
   Now for their deliv'rance rise.

2 Lo! with deep contrition turning,
   In Thy holy place we bend;
   Hear us, fasting, praying, mourning;
   Hear us, spare us, and defend.

3 Though our sins, our hearts confounding,
   Long and loud for vengeance call,
   Thou hast mercy more abounding;
   Jesus' blood can cleanse them all.

4 Let that mercy veil transgression;
   Let that blood our guilt efface:
   Save Thy people from oppression;
   Save from spoil Thy holy place.

C. F., 1804.

BpC	940
BpN	om
BpS	om
CoA	591
CoC	om
CoR	om
CoS	1119
Dis	om
Ep	310
EAs	om
LuC	495
LuS	540
MEN	1081
MES	om
Mor	267
PrN	840
PrS	om
RAm	895
RUS	om
RfE	240
UBr	om
BCh	om
Hat	om
HES	om
HEM	om
HSP	543
H&L	om
LWB	om
RSS	om
RLD	om

ST. PETERSBURGH. L. M. Dimitri Bortniansky, 1826.

1 When gathering clouds around I view,
And days are dark, and friends are few,
On Him I lean, Who not in vain
Experienced every human pain:
He sees my wants, allays my fears,
And counts and treasures up my tears.

2 If aught should tempt my soul to stray
From heavenly wisdom's narrow way,
To fly the good I would pursue,
Or do the ill I would not do;
Still He who felt temptation's power
Will guard me in that dangerous hour.

3 If vexing thoughts within me rise,
And sore dismayed, my spirit dies,—
Still He, Who once vouchsafed to bear
The sickening anguish of despair,
Shall sweetly soothe, shall gently dry,
The throbbing heart, the streaming eye.

4 When sorrowing o'er some stone I bend,
Which covers what was once a friend,
And from his hand, his voice, his smile,
Divides me for a little while;
Thou, Saviour, seest the tears I shed,
For Thou didst weep o'er Lazarus dead.

5 And, O! when I have safely passed
Through every conflict but the last,
Still, still unchanging watch beside
My painful bed, for Thou hast died;
Then point to realms of cloudless day,
And wipe the latest tear away.

Sir Robert Grant, 1806.

BpC	655
BpN	122
BpS	983
CoA	om
CoC	517
CoR	321
CoS	412
Dis	om
Ep	250
EAs	om
LuC	212
LuS	om
MEN	om
MES	734
Mor	532
PrN	282
PrS	60
RAm	612
RUS	387
RfE	243
UBr	om
BCh	136
Hat	1067
HES	301
HEM	517
HSP	om
H&L	411
LWB	178
RSS	708
RLD	881

LYONS. 10s, 11.

F. JOS. HAYDN, 1709.

1. O worship the King, all-glorious above,
   And gratefully sing His wonderful love;
   Our Shield and Defender, the Ancient of days,
   Pavilioned in splendor, and girded with praise.

2. O tell of His might, and sing of His grace,
   Whose robe is the light, whose canopy space;
   His chariots of wrath the deep thunder-clouds form,
   And dark is His path on the wings of the storm.

3. The earth with its store of wonders untold,
   Almighty, Thy power hath founded of old,
   Hath stablished it fast by a changeless decree,
   And round it hath cast, like a mantle, the sea.

4. Thy bountiful care what tongue can recite?
   It breathes in the air, it shines in the light,
   It streams from the hills, it descends to the plain,
   And sweetly distills in the dew and the rain.

5. Frail children of dust, and feeble as frail,
   In Thee do we trust, nor find Thee to fail;
   Thy mercies how tender, how firm to the end,
   Our Maker, Defender, Redeemer and Friend.

6. O measureless Might! ineffable Love!
   While angels delight to hymn Thee above,
   The humbler creation, though feeble their lays,
   With true adoration shall lisp to Thy praise.

   Sir Robert Grant, 1830.

BpC	112
BpN	1
BpS	257
CoA	15
CoC	140
CoR	125
CoS	115
Dis	163
Ep	519
EAs	34
LuC	om
LuS	55
MEN	140
MES	47
Mor	om
PrN	362
PrS	430
RAm	172
RUS	406
RfE	302
UBr	om
BCh	82
Hat	262
HES	56
HEM	2
HSP	1460
H&L	85
LWB	124
RSS	98
RLD	143

LISCHER. H. M.   Arr. by LOWELL MASON, 1841.

1 Awake, ye saints! awake,
   And hail this sacred day;
 In loftiest songs of praise
   Your joyful homage pay:
 Come, bless the day that God hath blessed,
 The type of heaven's eternal rest.

2 On this auspicious morn,
   The Lord of life arose;
 He burst the bars of death,
   And vanquished all our foes;
 And now he pleads our cause above,
 And reaps the fruit of all his love.

3 All hail, triumphant Lord!
   Heaven with hosannas rings;
 And earth, in humbler strains,
   Thy praise responsive sings:
 Worthy the Lamb that once was slain,
 Through endless years to live and reign.

    Elizabeth Scott, 1793. Rev. Thomas Cotterill, 1810.

BpC	om
BpN	om
BpS	9
CoA	om
CoC	om
CoR	om
CoS	58
Dis	147
Ep	148
EAs	604
LuC	om
LuS	37
MEN	73
MES	om
Mor	om
PrN	om
PrS	796
RAm	12
RUS	om
RfE	152
UBr	99
BCh	om
Hat	64
HES	om
HEM	om
HSP	1014
H&L	om
LWB	om
RSS	om
RLD	74

GRACE CHURCH. L. M.
IGNAZ PLEYEL, 1831.

1 Father of Heaven, Whose love profound
A ransom for our souls hath found,
Before Thy throne we sinners bend;
To us Thy pardoning love extend.

2 Almighty Son, incarnate Word,
Our Prophet, Priest, Redeemer, Lord,
Before Thy throne we sinners bend;
To us Thy saving grace extend.

3 Eternal Spirit, by Whose breath
The soul is raised from sin and death,
Before Thy throne we sinners bend;
To us Thy quickening power extend.

4 Jehovah—Father, Spirit, Son—
Mysterious Godhead, Three in One!
Before Thy Throne we sinners bend;
Grace, pardon, life to us extend.

Rev. Edward Cooper, 1805.

BpC	104
BpN	212
BpS	110
CoA	352
CoC	om
CoR	om
CoS	471
Dis	om
Ep	142
EAs	3
LuC	263
LuS	63
MEN	35
MES	om
Mor	311
PrN	71
PrS	om
RAm	98
RUS	om
RfE	om
UBr	393
BCh	5
Hat	137
HES	8
HEM	109
HSP	om
H&L	om
LWB	om
RSS	247
RLD	170

JUDGMENT HYMN. P. M.
JOSEPH KLUG, 1535.

JUDGMENT HYMN. P. M. Concluded.

1 Great God, what do I see and hear!
    The end of things created!
  The Judge of mankind doth appear
    On clouds of glory seated!
  The trumpet sounds; the graves restore
  The dead which they contained before:
    Prepare, my soul, to meet Him.

2 The dead in Christ shall first arise
    At the last trumpet's sounding,
  Caught to meet Him in the skies,
    With joy their Lord surrounding:
  No gloomy fears their souls dismay;
  His presence sheds eternal day
    On those prepared to meet Him.

3 But sinners, filled with guilty fears,
    Behold His wrath prevailing:
  For they shall rise, and find their tears
    And sighs are unavailing;
  The day of grace is past and gone;
  Trembling they stand before the throne,
    All unprepared to meet Him.

4 Great God, what do I see and hear,
    The end of things created!
  The Judge of man I see appear,
    On clouds of glory seated;
  Beneath His cross I view the day,
  When heaven and earth shall pass away,
    And thus prepare to meet Him.

Vs. 2-4: Rev. William Bengo Collyer, 1812.
Rev. Thos. Cotterill, 1819.

BpC	1023
BpN	660
BpS	om
CoA	168
CoC	873
CoR	om
CoS	1284
Dis	om
Ep	484
EAs	845
LuC	565
LuS	om
MEN	1028
MES	om
Mor	748
PrN	764
PrS	om
RAm	957
RUS	21
RfE	483
UBr	om
BCh	587
Hat	140
HES	347
HEM	om
HSP	720
H&L	485
LWB	233
RSS	1247
RLD	976

STELLA. L. M.
JAMES MILLAR, 1754.

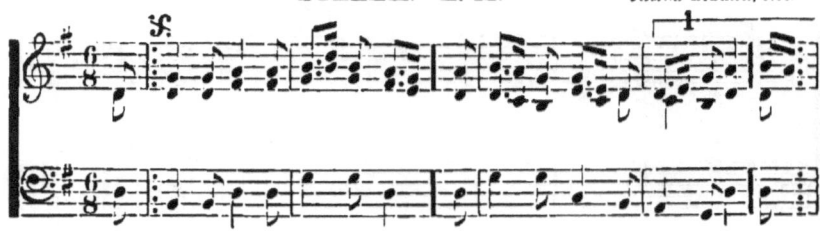

1 When marshall'd on the nightly plain,
     The glittering host bestud the sky,
   One star alone, of all the train,
     Can fix the sinner's wandering eye.
   Hark! hark! to God the chorus breaks,
     From ev'ry host, from ev'ry gem;
   But one alone the Saviour speaks—
     It is the Star of Bethlehem.

2 Once on the raging seas I rode,
     The storm was loud, the night was dark;
   The ocean yawned, and rudely blowed
     The wind that tossed my foundering bark.
   Deep horror then my vitals froze,
     Death-struck, I ceased the tide to stem;
   When suddenly a Star arose—
     It was the Star of Bethlehem.

3 It was my guide, my light, my all;
     It bade my dark forebodings cease;
   And through the storm, and danger's thrall,
     It led me to the port of peace.
   Now safely moored—my perils o'er,
     I'll sing, first in night's diadem,
   Forever and forevermore,
     The Star— the Star of Bethlehem!

Henry Kirke White, (1806,) 1812.

BpC 342
BpN 154
BpS 291
CoA om
CoC 472
CoR 222
CoS 428
Dis om
Ep 46
EAs 88
LuC om
LuS 171
MEN 187
MES 691
Mor om
PrN 103
PrS 127
RAm om
RUS 87
RfE 40
UBr 212

BCh 130
Hat 416
HES 187
HEM 166
HSP om
H&L 212
LWB om
RSS 241
RLD 315

DRESDEN. 6 or 8 lines. Arr. Aaron Williams, cir. 1760.

1 When, streaming from the eastern skies,
  The morning light salutes mine eyes,
  O Sun of Righteousness divine,
  On me with beams of mercy shine!
  Oh! chase the clouds of guilt away,
  And turn my darkness into day.

2 And when to heaven's all-glorious King
  My morning sacrifice I bring,
  And, mourning o'er my guilt and shame,
  Ask mercy in my Saviour's name;
  Then, Jesus, cleanse me with Thy blood,
  And be my Advocate with God.

3 As every day Thy mercy spares,
  Will bring its trials and its cares;
  O Saviour, till my life shall end,
  Be Thou my counsellor and friend:
  Teach me Thy precepts, all divine,
  And be Thy great example mine.

4 When each day's scenes and labors close,
  And wearied nature seeks repose,
  With pardoning mercy richly blest,
  Guard me, my Saviour, while I rest;
  And, as each morning sun shall rise,
  Oh, lead me onward to the skies!

5 And at my life's last setting sun,
  My conflicts o'er, my labors done,
  Jesus, Thy heavenly radiance shed,
  To cheer and bless my dying-bed;
  And from death's gloom my spirit raise,
  To see Thy face, and sing Thy praise.

William Shrubsole, 1813.

BpC	77
BpN	53
BpS	26
CoA	om
CoC	om
CoR	41
CoS	47
Dis	om
Ep	314
EAs	om
LuC	507
LuS	513
MEN	110
MES	om
Mor	671
PrN	894
PrS	om
RAm	835
RUS	om
RfE	om
UBr	om
BCh	250
Hat	5
HES	99
HEM	20
HSP	om
H&L	4
LWB	145
RSS	9
RLD	200

115

MISSIONARY HYMN. 7s & 6s. D. — LOWELL MASON, 1824.

7s & 6s. Double.

1 From Greenland's icy mountains,
　　From India's coral strand,
　Where Afric's sunny fountains
　　Roll down their golden sand;
　From many an ancient river,
　　From many a palmy plain,
　They call us to deliver
　　Their land from error's chain.

2 What though the spicy breezes
　　Blow soft o'er Ceylon's isle;
　Though every prospect pleases,
　　And only man is vile:
　In vain with lavish kindness
　　The gifts of God are strown;
　The heathen in his blindness
　　Bows down to wood and stone.

3 Can we, whose souls are lighted
　　With wisdom from on high,
　Can we to men benighted
　　The lamp of life deny?
　Salvation! O salvation!
　　The joyful sound proclaim,
　Till each remotest nation
　　Has learnt Messiah's name.

4 Waft, waft, ye winds, His story,
　　And you, ye waters, roll,
　Till like a sea of glory
　　It spreads from pole to pole;
　Till o'er our ransomed nature
　　The Lamb for sinners slain,
　Redeemer, King, Creator,
　　In bliss returns to reign.

　　　　　Rt. Rev. Reginald Heber, 1819.

BpC	927
BpN	605
BpS	1233
CoA	296
CoC	820
CoR	541
CoS	1132
Dis	662
Ep	283
EAs	688
LuC	297
LuS	221
MEN	930
MES	615
Mor	828
PrN	645
PrS	603
RAm	808
RUS	133
RfE	287
UBr	1061
BCh	520
Hat	1242
HES	1119
HEM	627
HSP	779
H&L	472
LWB	444
RSS	890
RLD	1061

SILOAM. C. M.
ISAAC B. WOODBURY, 1850.

1. By cool Siloam's shady rill
   How fair the lily grows!
   How sweet the breath, beneath the hill,
   Of Sharon's dewy rose!

2. Lo! such the child whose early feet
   The paths of peace have trod,
   Whose secret heart, with influence sweet,
   Is upward drawn to God.

3. By cool Siloam's shady rill
   The lily must decay;
   The rose that blooms beneath the hill
   Must shortly fade away.

4. And soon, too soon, the wintry hour
   Of man's maturer age
   Will shake the soul with sorrow's power,
   And stormy passion's rage.

5. O thou who givest life and breath,
   We seek Thy grace alone,
   In childhood, manhood, age, and death,
   To keep us still Thine own.

Rt. Rev. Reg. Heber, 1827.

BpC	881
BpN	572
BpS	585
CoA	223
CoC	762
CoR	518
CoS	1089
Dis	om
Ep	224
EAs	750
LuC	om
LuS	507
MEN	875
MES	647
Mor	1448
PrN	657
PrS	522
RAm	723
RUS	498
RfE	om
UBr	1180
BCh	502
Hat	om
HES	1176
HEM	563
HSP	om
H&L	563
LWB	om
RSS	810
RLD	954

FOLSOM. 11s & 10s.
J. C. W. A. MOZART, (? 1791.)

1 Brightest and best of the sons of the morning!
  Dawn on our darkness, and lend us thine aid;
  Star of the East, the horizon adorning,
  Guide where our infant Redeemer is laid.

2 Cold on His cradle the dew-drops are shining;
  Low lies His head with the beasts of the stall:
  Angels adore Him in slumber reclining,
  Maker, and Monarch, and Saviour of all!

3 Say, shall we yield Him, in costly devotion,
  Odors of Edom, and offerings divine?
  Gems of the mountain, and pearls of the ocean,
  Myrrh from the forest, or gold from the mine?

4 Vainly we offer each ample oblation,
  Vainly with gold would His favors secure:
  Richer, by far, is the heart's adoration;
  Dearer to God are the prayers of the poor.

5 Brightest and best of the sons of the morning!
  Dawn on our darkness, and lend us thine aid;
  Star of the East, the horizon adorning,
  Guide where our infant Redeemer is laid.

Rt. Rev. Reginald Heber, 1811.

BpC 219
BpN 113
BpS 298
CoA 56
CoC 164
CoR 166
CoS 266
Dis om
Ed 37
EAs 92
LuC om
LuS 170
MEN 186
MES 61
Mor 1150
PrN 108
PrS 69
RAm 190
RUS 76
RfE 46
UBr 226
BCh 83
Hat 415
HES 183
HEM 161
HSP 1449
H&L 203
LWB 174
RSS 250
RLD 335

WILMOT. 8s, 7s. C. M. VON WEBER. Arr. by L. MASON.

1 Hark what mean those holy voices,
　　Sweetly sounding through the skies?
　Lo! the angelic host rejoices,
　　Heavenly hallelujahs rise.
　Listen to the wondrous story
　　Which they chant in hymns of joy:
　" Glory in the highest, glory!
　　Glory be to God most high!

2 "Peace on earth, good-will from heaven
　　Reaching far as man is found;
　Souls redeemed and sins forgiven;—
　　Loud our golden harps shall sound.
　Christ is born, the great Anointed:
　　Heaven and earth His praises sing!
　O receive whom God appointed
　　For your Prophet, Priest and King!

3 "Hasten, mortals, to adore Him;
　　Learn His name and taste His joy:
　Till in heaven ye sing before Him,
　　Glory be to God most high!"
　Let us learn the wondrous story
　　Of our great Redeemer's birth;
　Spread the brightness of its glory
　　Till it cover all the earth.

　　　　　　　　Rev. John Cawood, 1819.

```
BpC  216
BpN  109
BpS  269
CoA   51
CoC  169
CoR  162
CoS  269
Dis   om
Ep    20
EAs   91
LuC  127
LuS  229
MEN  188
MES   om
Mor  274
PrN  113
PrS   74
RAm  196
RUS   69
RfE   24
UBr  222

BCh   om
Hat  409
HES  164
HEM  172
HSP  824
H&L  190
LWB   om
RSS  234
RLD  334
```

STATE STREET. S. M. JONATHAN C. WOODMAN, 1844.

1 Lord God, the Holy Ghost,
　In this accepted hour,
As on the day of Pentecost,
　Descend in all Thy power.

2 We meet with one accord
　In our appointed place,
And wait the promise of our Lord,
　The Spirit of all grace.

3 Like mighty rushing wind
　Upon the waves beneath,
Move with one impulse every mind,
　One soul, one feeling breathe.

4 The young, the old inspire
　With wisdom from above;
And give us hearts and tongues of fire
　To pray, and praise, and love.

5 Spirit of light, explore
　And chase our gloom away,
With lustre shining more and more
　Unto the perfect day.

6 Spirit of truth, be Thou,
　In life and death, our guide;
O Spirit of adoption, now
　May we be sanctified.

　　　　James Montgomery, 1819.

BpC	382
BpN	om
BpS	534
CoA	om
CoC	om
CoR	om
CoS	448
Dis	om
Ep	130
EAs	165
LuC	241
LuS	248
MEN	286
MES	145
Mor	1484
PrN	494
PrS	746
RAm	367
RUS	om
RfE	130
UBr	379
BCh	133
Hat	335
HES	349
HEM	276
HSP	om
H&L	267
LWB	om
RSS	om
RLD	526

BYEFIELD. C. M. THOMAS HASTINGS, 1840.

1 Prayer is the soul's sincere desire,
  Uttered or unexpressed;
  The motion of a hidden fire
  That trembles in the breast.

2 Prayer is the burden of a sigh,
  The falling of a tear,
  The upward glancing of an eye
  When none but God is near.

3 Prayer is the simplest form of speech
  That infant lips can try;
  Prayer the sublimest strains that reach
  The Majesty on high.

4 Prayer is the contrite sinner's voice
  Returning from his ways,
  While angels in their songs rejoice,
  And cry, "Behold, he prays!"

5 Prayer is the Christian's vital breath,
  The Christian's native air,
  His watchword at the gates of death—
  He enters heaven with prayer.

6 O Thou, by whom we come to God,
  The Life, the Truth, the Way,
  The path of prayer Thyself hast trod;
  Lord, teach us how to pray.

James Montgomery, 1818.

BpC 629
BpN 396
BpS 65
CoA 470
CoC 675
CoR 405
CoS 856
Dis om
Ep 404
EAs 404
LuC om
LuS 326
MEN 710
MES 722
Mor 157
PrN 350
PrS 364
RAm 690
RUS om
RfE 386
UBr 781

BCh 383
Hat 933
HES 808
HEM 523
HSP om
H&L 335
LWB om
RSS 67
RLD 112

REGENT SQUARE. 8s & 7s. 6 lines. HENRY SMART. 1867.

1 Angels, from the realms of glory,
   Wing your flight o'er all the earth;
  Ye who sang creation's story,
   Now proclaim Messiah's birth;
    Come and worship,
    Worship Christ the new-born King.

2 Shepherds, in the field abiding,
   Watching o'er your flocks by night,
  God with man is now residing;
   Yonder shines the infant Light;
    Come and worship,
    Worship Christ the new-born King.

3 Sages, leave your contemplations,
   Brighter visions beam afar;
  Seek the great Desire of nations;
   Ye have seen His natal star;
    Come and worship,
    Worship Christ the new-born King.

4 Saints, before the altar bending,
   Watching long in hope and fear,
  Suddenly the Lord, descending,
   In His temple shall appear;
    Come and worship,
    Worship Christ the new-born King.

5 Sinner, wrung with true repentance,
   Doomed for guilt to endless pains,
  Justice now revokes the sentence;
   Mercy calls you; break your chains;
    Come and worship,
    Worship Christ the new-born King.

                    James Montgomery, 1816.

BpC	218
BpN	om
BpS	271
CoA	57
CoC	om
CoR	om
CoS	om
Dis	om
Ep	24
EAs	om
LuC	om
LuS	234
MEN	189
MES	56
Mor	1386
PrN	om
PrS	713
RAm	189
RUS	79
RfE	26
UBr	225
BCh	om
Hat	413
HES	181
HEM	169
HSP	om
H&L	om
LWB	173
RSS	om
RLD	329

DENNIS. S. M. HANS GEORGE NAGELI, († 1836.)

1 Oh, where shall rest be found—
  Rest for the weary soul?
'Twere vain the ocean depths to sound,
  Or pierce to either pole.

2 The world can never give
  The bliss for which we sigh:
'Tis not the whole of life to live,
  Nor all of death to die.

3 Beyond this vale of tears
  There is a life above,
Unmeasured by the flight of years;
  And all that life is love.

4 There is a death whose pang
  Outlasts the fleeting breath:
Oh, what eternal horrors hang
  Around the second death!

5 Lord God of truth and grace,
  Teach us that death to shun;
Lest we be banished from Thy face,
  And evermore undone.

6 Here would we end our quest;
  Alone are found in Thee
The life of perfect love—the rest
  Of immortality.

James Montgomery, 1818.

BpC 471
BpN 634
BpS 605
CoA om
CoC 308
CoR om
CoS 496
Dis 449
Ep 513
EAs 237
LuC 96
LuS 480
MEN 358
MES 589
Mor 1343
PrN 767
PrS 311
RAm 383
RUS 28
RfE om
UBr 504

BCh 313
Hat 607
HES 462
HEM 314
HSP om
H&L om
LWB 254
RSS 381
RLD 556

ELTHAM. 7s. D. LOWELL MASON, 1840.

1 Hark the song of Jubilee,
  Loud as mighty thunders roar,
Or the fulness of the sea
  When it breaks upon the shore:
Hallelujah! for the Lord
  God omnipotent shall reign;
Hallelujah! let the word
  Echo round the earth and main.

2 Hallelujah! hark the sound
  From the depths unto the skies,
Wakes above, beneath, around,
  All creation's harmonies:
See Jehovah's banner furled,
  Sheathed His sword: He speaks—'tis done!
And the kingdoms of this world
  Are the kingdoms of His Son.

3 He shall reign from pole to pole
  With illimitable sway;
He shall reign when, like a scroll,
  Yonder heavens have passed away:
Then the end: beneath His rod
  Man's last enemy shall fall;
Hallelujah! Christ in God,
  God in Christ, is all in all.

James Montgomery, 1818.

BpC   om
BpN   603
BpS   1238
CoA   297
CoC   801
CoR   555
CoS   392
Dis   om
Ep   42
EAs   om
LuC   304
LuS   215
MEN   938
MES   623
Mor   1051
PrN   729
PrS   608
RAm   817
RUS   57
RfE   404
UBr   919

BCh   535
Hat   1120
HES   1141
HEM   648
HSP   1100
H&L   466
LWB   229
RSS   902
RLD   511

125

TELEMANN'S CHANT. 7s.

CHAS. ZEUNER, 1832.

1. Songs of praise the angels sang,
   Heaven with hallelujahs rang,
   When Jehovah's work begun,
   When He spake, and it was done.

2. Songs of praise awoke the morn,
   When the Prince of Peace was born:
   Songs of praise arose, when He
   Captive led captivity.

3. Heaven and earth must pass away;
   Songs of praise shall crown that day:
   God will make new heavens and earth;
   Songs of praise shall hail their birth.

4. And shall man alone be dumb
   Till that glorious kingdom come?
   No; the Church delights to raise
   Psalms, and hymns, and songs of praise.

5. Saints below, with heart and voice,
   Still in songs of praise rejoice;
   Learning here, by faith and love,
   Songs of praise to sing above.

6. Borne upon their latest breath
   Songs of praise shall conquer death;
   Then, amid eternal joy,
   Songs of praise their powers employ.

James Montgomery, 1819.

BpC	131
BpN	172
BpS	243
CoA	204
CoC	193
CoR	129
CoS	25
Dis	om
Ep	422
EAs	om
LuC	13
LuS	om
MEN	24
MES	om
Mor	49
PrN	17
PrS	om
RAm	154
RUS	59
RfE	om
UBr	49
BCh	81
Hat	258
HES	68
HEM	119
HSP	om
H&L	510
LWB	om
RSS	107
RLD	148

BEULAH. 7s. Double.   ELAM IVES, Jr., 1836.

1 What are these in bright array,
    This innumerable throng,
  Round the altar, night and day,
    Hymning one triumphant song?—
  "Worthy is the Lamb once slain,
    Blessing, honor, glory, power,
  Wisdom, riches to obtain,
    New dominion every hour!"

2 These through fiery trials trod;
    These from great affliction came;
  Now before the throne of God,
    Sealed with His almighty name,
  Clad in raiment pure and white,
    Victor-palms in every hand,
  Through their dear Redeemer's might,
    More than conquerors they stand.

3 Hunger, thirst, disease unknown,
    On immortal fruits they feed;
  Them the Lamb amidst the throne
    Shall to living fountains lead:
  Joy and gladness banish sighs;
    Perfect love dispels all fear;
  And for ever from their eyes
    God shall wipe away the tear.

                    James Montgomery, 1819.

BpC 1063
BpN 676
BpS 1084
CoA 513
CoC 908
CoR 624
CoS 1248
Dis 487
Ep   494
EAs om
LuC 582
LuS 581
MEN om
MES 557
Mor 1059
PrN 800
PrS 677
RAm 764
RUS 746
RfE 496
UBr om

BCh 604
Hat 1412
HES 1366
HEM 712
HSP om
H&L 502
LWB 391
RSS 999
RLD om

GETHSEMANE. 7s. 6 Lines. RICHARD REDHEAD, 1853.

1 Go to dark Gethsemane,
   Ye that feel the tempter's power;
Your Redeemer's conflict see,
   Watch with Him one bitter hour:
Turn not from His griefs away,
Learn of Jesus Christ to pray.

2 Follow to the judgment-hall,
   View the Lord of life arraigned;
O the wormwood and the gall!
   O the pangs His soul sustained;
Shun not suffering, shame, or loss;
Learn of Him to bear the cross.

3 Calvary's mournful mountain climb;
   There, adoring at His feet,
Mark that miracle of time,
   God's own sacrifice complete:
"It is finished," hear Him cry;
Learn of Jesus Christ to die.

4 Early hasten to the tomb,
   Where they laid His breathless clay:
All is solitude and gloom;
   Who hath taken Him away?
Christ is risen; he meets our eyes;
Saviour, teach us so to rise.

James Montgomery, 1820, 1825.

BpC	239
BpN	om
BpS	362
CoA	87
CoC	729
CoR	om
CoS	290
Dis	656
Ep	86
EAs	124
LuC	173
LuS	120
MEN	223
MES	om
Mor	1250
PrN	138
PrS	76
RAm	270
RUS	247
RfE	78
UBr	om
BCh	95
Hat	442
HES	226
HEM	191
HSP	1125
H&L	229
LWB	om
RSS	om
RLD	403

MELCOMBE. SAMUEL WEBBE, 1800.

1 O Spirit of the living God,
   In all Thy plenitude of grace,
   Where'er the foot of man hath trod,
   Descend on our apostate race.

2 Give tongues of fire and hearts of love
   To preach the reconciling word;
   Give power and unction from above,
   Where'er the joyful sound is heard.

3 Be darkness at Thy coming light,
   Confusion order in Thy path:
   Souls without strength inspire with might,
   Bid mercy triumph over wrath.

4 Baptize the nations; far and nigh
   The triumph of the Cross record;
   The name of Jesus glorify
   Till every kindred call Him Lord.

James Montgomery, 1823.

BpC 91
BpN om
BpS 1205
CoA 180
CoC 783
CoR om
CoS om
Dis om
Ep 120
EAs om
LuC 300
LuS 190
MEN 276
MES 157
Mor 401
PrN 616
PrS 598
RAm 708
RUS 325
RfE 209
UBr 1035
BCh 528
Hat 1222
HES 1067
HEM 621
HSP om
H&L 265
LWB 245
RSS 380
RLD om

WEBB. 7s & 6s. GEO. JAMES WEBB, 1837.

1 Hail to the Lord's Anointed,
   Great David's greater Son!
  Hail, in the time appointed,
   His reign on earth begun!
  He comes to break oppression,
   To set the captive free,
  To take away transgression,
   And rule in equity.

2 He comes with succor speedy
   To those who suffer wrong,
  To help the poor and needy,
   And bid the weak be strong:
  To give them songs for sighing,
   Their darkness turn to light,
  Whose souls, condemned and dying,
   Were precious in His sight.

BpC	914
BpN	112
BpS	294
CoA	282
CoC	823
CoR	om
CoS	1039
Dis	139
Ep	34
EAs	692
LuC	122
LuS	153
MEN	181
MES	om
Mor	801
PrN	646
PrS	om
RAm	804
RUS	98
RfE	42
UBr	927
BCh	536
Hut	1109
HES	1122
HEM	628
HSP	om
H&L	476
LWB	49
RSS	894
RLD	1065

7s & 6s. D.

3 He shall come down like showers
　　Upon the fruitful earth,
And love, joy, hope, like flowers,
　　Spring in His path to birth:
Before Him, on the mountains,
　　Shall Peace the herald go;
And righteousness in fountains
　　From hill to valley flow.

4 Kings shall fall down before Him,
　　And gold and incense bring;
All nations shall adore Him,
　　His praise all people sing:
For He shall have dominion
　　O'er river, sea and shore,
Far as the eagle's pinion
　　Or dove's light wing can soar.

5 For Him shall prayer unceasing
　　And daily vows ascend,
His kingdom still increasing,
　　A kingdom without end:
The mountain-dews shall nourish
　　A seed in weakness sown,
Whose fruit shall spread and flourish
　　And shake like Lebanon.

6 O'er every foe victorious
　　He on His throne shall rest,
From age to age more glorious,
　　All-blessing and all-blest;
The tide of time shall never
　　His covenant remove:
His name shall stand forever;
　　That name to us is Love!

　　　　　　　　James Montgomery, 1821.

LISBON. S. M.   DANIEL READ, 1785.

1 Sow in the morn thy seed,
   At eve hold not thy hand;
To doubt and fear give thou no heed;
   Broadcast it o'er the land.

2 And duly shall appear,
   In verdure, beauty, strength,
The tender blade, the stalk, the ear,
   And the full corn at length.

3 Thou canst not toil in vain;
   Cold, heat, and moist, and dry,
Shall foster and mature the grain
   For garners in the sky.

4 Thence, when the glorious end,
   The day of God, shall come,
The angel reapers shall descend,
   And heaven cry "Harvest-home!"

James Montgomery, 1832.

BpC	om
BpN	469
BpS	923
CoA	271
CoC	573
CoR	om
CoS	881
Dis	440
Ep	298
EAs	550
LuC	om
LuS	432
MEN	575
MES	467
Mor	1360
PrN	om
PrS	256
RAm	om
RUS	555
RfE	om
UBr	1014
BCh	om
Hut	1262
HES	853
HEM	om
HSP	537
H&L	om
LWB	om
RSS	782
RLD	904

AVON. C. M. HUGH WILSON, (xviii Cent.)

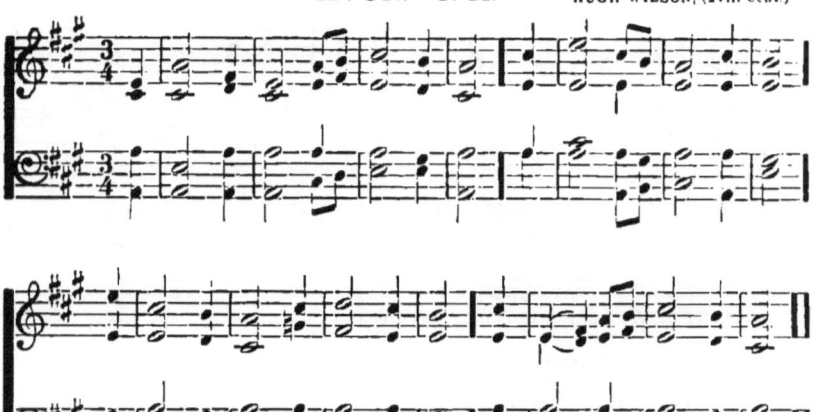

1 According to Thy gracious word,
  In meek humility,
This will I do, my dying Lord!
  I will remember Thee.

2 Thy body, broken for my sake,
  My bread from heaven shall be;
The testamental cup I take,
  And thus remember Thee.

3 Gethsamene can I forget?
  Or there Thy conflict see,
Thine agony and bloody sweat,
  And not remember Thee?

4 When to Thy cross I turn mine eyes
  And rest on Calvary,
O Lamb of God, my sacrifice!
  I must remember Thee:—

5 Remember Thee, and all Thy pains,
  And all Thy love to me;
Yea, while a breath, a pulse remains,
  Will I remember Thee.

6 And when these failing lips grow dumb,
  And mind and memory flee,
When Thou shalt in Thy kingdom come,
  Then, Lord, remember me.

James Montgomery, 1825.

BpC	839
BpN	om
BpS	om
CoA	242
CoC	731
CoR	525
CoS	1050
Dis	om
Ep	211
EAs	664
LuC	328
LuS	261
MEN	836
MES	213
Mor	172
PrN	681
PrS	553
RAm	734
RUS	539
RfE	195
UBr	om
BCh	506
Hat	744
HES	905
HEM	587
HSP	1387
H&L	444
LWB	505
RSS	862
RLD	992

OLMUTZ. S. M.
GREGORIAN. Arr. by LOWELL MASON, 1832.

1 "Forever with the Lord!"
   Amen! so let it be!
   Life from the dead is in that word,
   'Tis immortality.

2 Here in the body pent,
   Absent from Him I roam,
   Yet nightly pitch my moving tent
   A day's march nearer home.

3 My Father's house on high,
   Home of my soul! how near
   At times to faith's foreseeing eye,
   Thy golden gates appear!

4 Ah, then my spirit faints
   To reach the land I love,
   The bright inheritance of saints,
   Jerusalem above!

5 "Forever with the Lord!"
   Father, if 'tis Thy will,
   The promise of that faithful word
   E'en here to me fulfil.

6 Be Thou at my right hand;
   Then can I never fail:
   Uphold Thou me, and I shall stand;
   Fight, and I must prevail.

7 So when my latest breath
   Shall rend the veil in twain,
   By death I shall escape from death,
   And life eternal gain.

8 Knowing as I am known,
   How shall I love that word,
   And oft repeat before the throne:
   "Forever with the Lord!"

James Montgomery, 1835.

BpC 1051
BpN 666
BpS 1133
CoA 518
CoC 853
CoR 598
CoS 1237
Dis 106
Ep 489
EAs 820
LuC 585
LuS 588
MEN 1050
MES 562
Mor 1303
PrN 758
PrS 695
RAm 939
RUS 27
RfE 502
UBr 1134

BCh 598
Hat 1375
HES 1334
HEM 674
HSP om
H&L 451
LWB 410
RSS 946
RLD 1097

ORTONVILLE. C. M.
THOMAS HASTINGS, 1837.

1 The head that once was crowned with thorns,
   Is crowned with glory now;
   A royal diadem adorns
     The mighty victor's brow.

2 The highest place that heaven affords
   Is His, is His by right,
   The King of kings, and Lord of lords,
     And heaven's eternal Light.

3 The joy of all who dwell above,
   The joy of all below,
   To whom He manifests His love,
     And grants His name to know.

4 To them the cross, with all its shame,
   With all its grace, is given;
   Their name an everlasting name,
     Their joy the joy of heaven.

5 They suffer with their Lord below,
   They reign with Him above,
   Their profit and their joy to know
     The mystery of His love.

6 The cross He bore is life and health,
   Though shame and death to Him;
   His people's hope, His people's wealth,
     Their everlasting theme.
                  Rev. Thomas Kelly, 1820.

BpC	302
BpN	141
BpS	390
CoA	124
CoC	208
CoR	210
CoS	om
Dis	om
Ep	114
EAs	134
LuC	205
LuS	om
MEN	256
MES	om
Mor	om
PrN	168
PrS	124
RAm	315
RUS	286
RfE	om
UBr	337
BCh	121
Hat	529
HES	302
HEM	235
HSP	478
H&L	129
LWB	om
RSS	328
RLD	460

12s.

1 The voice of free grace cries,
    Escape to the mountain,
For Adam's lost race
    Christ hath opened a fountain;
For sin and uncleanness,
    And every transgression,
His blood flows most freely
    In streams of salvation.
Hallelujah to the Lamb,
    Who hath purchased our pardon,
We'll praise Him again
    When we pass over Jordan.

2 Ye souls that are wounded!
    Oh, flee to the Saviour!
He calls you in mercy,
    'Tis infinite favor;
Your sins are increasing,
    Escape to the mountain—
His blood can remove them,
    It flows from the fountain.
Hallelujah to the Lamb, etc.

3 O Jesus! ride onward,
    Triumphantly glorious!
O'er sin, death, and hell,
    Thou art more than victorious;
Thy name is the theme
    Of the great congregation,
While angels and men
    Raise the shout of salvation.
Hallelujah to the Lamb, etc.

4 With joy shall we stand,
    When escaped to the shore;
With harps in our hands,
    We'll praise Him the more;
We'll range the sweet plains
    On the banks of the river,
And sing of salvation
    For ever and ever.
Hallelujah to the Lamb, etc.

            Richard Burdsall, 1806, 1824.

BpC	om
BpN	om
BpS	642
CoA	om
CoC	328
CoR	om
CoS	521
Dis	om
Ep	384
EAs	om
LuC	om
LuS	281
MEN	330
MES	137
Mor	504
PrN	637
PrS	605
RAm	om
RUS	49
RfE	330
UBr	471
BCh	om
Hat	606
HES	411
HEM	296
HSP	om
H&L	om
LWB	om
RSS	402
RLD	om

ELLESDIE. 8s & 7s. D. Arr. from J. C. W. A. MOZART, 1756.

1 Jesus, I my cross have taken,
   All to leave, and follow Thee;
Destitute, despised, forsaken,
   Thou from hence my all shalt be:
Perish every fond ambition,
   All I've sought, and hoped, and known!
Yet how rich is my condition,
   God and heaven are still my own.

2 Let the world despise and leave me,
   They have left my Saviour too;
Human hearts and looks deceive me;
   Thou art not, like man, untrue:
And while Thou shalt smile upon me,
   God of wisdom, love and might,
Foes may hate, and friends may shun me,
   Show Thy face and all is bright.

BpC 679
BpN 455
BpS 705
CoA 368
CoC 368
CoR 295
CoS 966
Dis 687
Ep 236
EAs 349
LuC 444
LuS 424
MEN 643
MES 494
Mor 956
PrN 317
PrS 346
RAm 475
RUS 574
RfE 206
UBr 704

BCh 363
Hat 648
HES 610
HEM 444
HSP 1205
H&L 303
LWB 272
RSS 520
RLD 1023

8s & 7s. Double.

3 Go then, earthly fame and treasure!
    Come disaster, scorn and pain!
In Thy service pain is pleasure,
    With Thy favor loss is gain.
I have called Thee Abba Father;
    I have stayed my heart on Thee:
Storms may howl and clouds may gather,
    All must work for good to me.

4 Man may trouble and distress me,
    'Twill but drive me to Thy breast;
Life with trials hard may press me,
    Heaven will bring me sweeter rest.
Oh 'tis not in grief to harm me,
    While Thy love is left to me;
Oh 't were not in joy to charm me,
    Were that joy unmixed with Thee.

5 Take, my soul, thy full salvation,
    Rise o'er sin, and fear, and care;
Joy to find in every station
    Something still to do or bear.
Think what Spirit dwells within thee,
    What a Father's smile is thine,
What a Saviour died to win thee:
    Child of heaven, shouldst thou repine?

6 Haste then on from grace to glory,
    Armed by faith, and winged by prayer,
Heaven's eternal day's before thee,
    God's own hand shall guide thee there.
Soon shall close thy earthly mission,
    Swift shall pass thy pilgrim days,
Hope shall change to glad fruition,
    Faith to sight, and prayer to praise.

Rev. Henry Francis Lyte, 1824.

EVENTIDE. 10s.   WILLIAM HENRY MONK.

1 Abide with me! fast falls the eventide;
The darkness deepens; Lord, with me abide!
When other helpers fail, and comforts flee,
Help of the helpless, O abide with me!

2 Swift to its close ebbs out life's little day;
Earth's joys grow dim; its glories pass away;
Change and decay in all around I see;
O Thou, who changest not, abide with me!

3 I need Thy presence every passing hour:
What but Thy grace can foil the Tempter's power?
Who like Thyself my guide and stay can be?
Through cloud and sunshine, O abide with me!

4 I fear no foe, with Thee at hand to bless:
Ills have no weight, and tears no bitterness:
Where is death's sting? where, grave, thy victory?
I triumph still, if Thou abide with me!

5 Hold Thou Thy cross before my closing eyes!
Shine through the gloom, and point me to the skies!
Heaven's morning breaks, and earth's vain shadows
In life and death, O Lord, abide with me!   [flee;

Rev. Henry Francis Lyte, 1847.

```
BpC   392
BpN    89
BpS   973
CoA   578
CoC    77
CoR    40
CoS    om
Dis   564
Ep    335
EAs    44
LuC   517
LuS   532
MEN    93
MES   764
Mor   457
PrN   923
PrS   795
RAm   845
RUS   279
RfE   258
UBr    om
BCh   421
Hnt   909
HES  1024
HEM    55
HSP  1457
H&L    24
LWB   476
RSS   127
RLD   219
```

140

FIAT LUX. 6s, 4s.

J. B. DYKES.

1 Thou, Whose almighty word
Chaos and darkness heard,
　And took their flight;
Hear us, we humbly pray,
And, where the gospel's day
Sheds not its glorious ray,
　Let there be light!

2 Thou, Who didst come to bring,
On Thy redeeming wing,
　Healing and sight,
Health to the sick in mind,
Sight to the inly blind,
Oh, now to all mankind
　Let there be light!

3 Spirit of truth and love,
Life-giving, Holy Dove,
　Speed forth Thy flight;
Move on the waters' face,
Bearing the lamp of grace;
And in earth's darkest place
　Let there be light!

4 Blessèd and holy Three,
Glorious Trinity,
　Wisdom, Love, Might!
Boundless as ocean's tide,
Rolling in fullest pride,
Through the world far and wide,
　Let there be light!

Rev. John Marriott, 1813, 1825.

BpC	107
BpN	207
BpS	115
CoA	om
CoC	om
CoR	123
CoS	476
Dis	om
Ep	146
EAs	om
LuC	301
LuS	om
MEN	913
MES	om
Mor	1235
PrN	528
PrS	om
RAm	798
RUS	449
RfE	292
UBr	386
BCh	529
Hat	347
HES	3
HEM	638
HSP	1179
H&L	79
LWB	100
RSS	369
RLD	519

MORNING STAR. 7s. 8 lines.
LOWELL MASON, 1830.

1 Watchman, tell us of the night,
  What its signs of promise are.
  Traveler, o'er yon mountain's height,
  See that glory-beaming star!

2 Watchman, does its beauteous ray
  Aught of joy or hope foretell?
  Traveler, yes: it brings the day,
  Promised day of Israel.

3 Watchman, tell us of the night:
  Higher yet that star ascends.
  Traveler, blessedness and light,
  Peace and truth, its course portends.

4 Watchman, will its beams alone
  Gild the spot that gave them birth?
  Traveler, ages are its own:
  See! it bursts o'er all the earth!

5 Watchman, tell us of the night,
  For the morning seems to dawn.
  Traveler, darkness takes its flight,
  Doubt and terror are withdrawn.

6 Watchman, let thy wanderings cease;
  Hie thee to thy quiet home.
  Traveler, lo! the Prince of Peace,
  Lo! the Son of God is come!

Sir John Bowring, 1825.

BpC	221
BpN	659
BpS	123
CoA	285
CoC	800
CoR	537
CoS	276
Dis	481
Ep	43
EAs	700
LuC	om
LuS	217
MEN	935
MES	612
Mor	84
PrN	634
PrS	606
RAm	789
RUS	22
RfE	30
UBr	om
BCh	524
Hat	1211
HES	174
HEM	147
HSP	1105
H&L	om
LWB	om
RSS	932
RLD	510

FREDERICK. 11s. GEORGE KINGSLEY, 1838.

1 I would not live alway; I ask not to stay
Where storm after storm rises dark o'er the way:
The few lurid mornings that dawn on us here
Are enough for life's woes, full enough for its cheer.

2 I would not live alway, thus fettered by sin,
Temptation without and corruption within:
E'en the rapture of pardon is mingled with fears,
And the cup of thanksgiving with penitent tears.

3 I would not live alway; no, welcome the tomb;
Since Jesus hath lain there, I dread not its gloom:
There sweet be my rest, till He bid me arise
To hail Him in triumph descending the skies.

4 Who, who would live alway, away from his God?
Away from yon heaven, that blissful abode,
Where the rivers of pleasure flow o'er the bright plains,
And the noontide of glory eternally reigns:

5 Where the saints of all ages in harmony meet,
Their Saviour and brethren transported to greet,
While the anthems of rapture unceasingly roll,
And the smile of the Lord is the feast of the soul.

Rev. William Augustus Muhlenberg, 1826, 1859.

BpC 976
BpN 625
BpS 1113
CoA om
CoC 860
CoR 584
CoS 1176
Dis 569
Ep 93
EAs 829
LuC 542
Lus 471
MEN 998
MES 561
Mor 487
PrN 792
PrS 635
RAm 952
RUS 744
RfE 112
UBr om

BCh 569
Hat 1378
HES 1285
HEM 675
HSP om
H&L om
LWB 405
RSS 933
RLD om

SYCHAR. 8s & 7s.

J. B. DYKES, 1872.

1 Saviour, Who Thy flock art feeding
　With the Shepherd's kindest care,
All the feeble gently leading,
　While the lambs Thy bosom share,

2 Now, these little ones receiving,
　Fold them in Thy gracious arm;
There we know, Thy word believing,
　Only there, secure from harm.

3 Never, from Thy pasture roving,
　Let them be the lions' prey;
Let Thy tenderness so loving
　Keep them all life's dangerous way.

4 Then, within Thy fold eternal,
　Let them find a resting-place,
Feed in pastures ever vernal,
　Drink the rivers of Thy grace.

　　　　Rev. William Augustus Muhlenberg, 1826.

BpC　om
BpN　582
BpS　1283
CoA　225
CoC　om
CoR　517
CoS　om
Dis　om
Ep　213
EAs　676
LuC　532
LuS　258
MEN　888
MES　om
Mor　264
PrN　661
PrS　om
RAm　719
RUS　511
RfE　179
UBr　om

BCh　501
Hat　om
HES　871
HEM　558
HSP　om
H&L　575
LWB　om
RSS　817
RLD　950

HOLLEY. 7s.
GEORGE HEWS, 1835.

1 Softly now the light of day
  Fades upon my sight away;
  Free from care, from labor free,
  Lord, I would commune with Thee.

2 Thou, Whose all-pervading eye
  Naught escapes, without, within,
  Pardon each infirmity,
  Open fault and secret sin.

3 Soon for me the light of day
  Shall forever pass away;
  Then from sin and sorrow free,
  Take me, Lord, to dwell with Thee.

4 Thou, Who sinless yet hast known
  All of man's infirmity,
  Then from Thine eternal throne,
  Jesus, look with pitying eye.
          Rt. Rev. George W. Doane, 1826.

BpC 100
BpN 62
BpS 85
CoA 557
CoC 53
CoR 77
CoS om
Dis 462
Ep 340
EAs om
LuC 515
LuS 531
MEN 117
MES 767
Mor 70
PrN 918
PrS 453
RAm 856
RUS 640
RfE 266
UBr om

BCh 262
Hat 23
HES 1246
HEM 25
HSP om
H&L 21
LWB 479
RSS 129
RLD 191

COVENTRY. C. M. Dr. SAM. HOWARD (?), d. 1782.

1 Thou art the Way: to Thee alone
  From sin and death we flee;
  And he who would the Father seek,
  Must seek Him, Lord, by Thee.

2 Thou art the Truth: Thy word alone
  True wisdom can impart;
  Thou only canst instruct the mind,
  And purify the heart.

3 Thou art the Life: the rending tomb
  Proclaims Thy conquering arm;
  And those who put their trust in Thee
  Nor death nor hell shall harm.

4 Thou art the Way, the Truth, the Life:
  Grant us that Way to know;
  That Truth to keep; that Life to win,
  Whose joys eternal flow.

Rt. Rev. G. W. Doane, 1826.

BpC	339
BpN	115
BpS	319
CoA	om
CoC	268
CoR	om
CoS	445
Dis	376
Ep	501
EAs	97
LuC	228
LuS	106
MEN	318
MES	119
Mor	181
PrN	239
PrS	621
RAm	395
RUS	106
RfE	364
UBr	233
BCh	132
Hat	430
HES	304
HEM	260
HSP	968
H&L	216
LWB	163
RSS	265
RLD	352

OLNEY. S. M.

LOWELL MASON, 1830.

1 The Spirit, in our hearts,
   Is whispering, "Sinner, come;"
 The bride, the Church of Christ, proclaims
   To all His children, "Come!"

2 Let him that heareth say
   To all about him, "Come;"
 Let him that thirsts for righteousness,
   To Christ, the fountain, come!

3 Yes, whosoever will,
   Oh, let him freely come,
 And freely drink the stream of life;
   'T is Jesus bids him come.

4 Lo! Jesus, who invites,
   Declares, "I quickly come;"
 Lord, even so; we wait Thine hour;
   O blest Redeemer, come!

Rt. Rev. H. U. Onderdonk, 1826.

BpC om
BpN 262
BpS 596
CoA 335
CoC 303
CoR om
CoS 506
Dis om
Ep 134
EAs om
LuC 346
LuS 275
MEN 355
MES om
Mor 1330
PrN 563
PrS 179
RAm 385
RUS om
RfE 133
UBr 418

BCh 300
Hat 517
HES 442
HEM 307
HSP 559
H&L om
LWB 465
RSS 441
RLD 593

HURSLEY. L. M.
F. J. HAYDN. Arr. by W. H. MONK, 1861.

1 Sun of my soul! Thou Saviour dear,
It is not night if Thou be near:
Oh, may no earth-born cloud arise
To hide Thee from Thy servant's eyes!

2 When the soft dews of kindly sleep
My wearied eyelids gently steep,
Be my last thought,—how sweet to rest
For ever on my Saviour's breast!

3 Abide with me from morn till eve,
For without Thee I cannot live;
Abide with me when night is nigh,
For without Thee I dare not die.

4 If some poor wandering child of Thine
Have spurned to-day the voice divine,
Now, Lord, the gracious work begin;
Let him no more lie down in sin.

5 Watch by the sick; enrich the poor
With blessings from Thy boundless store;
Be every mourner's sleep to-night,
Like infant slumbers, pure and light.

6 Come near and bless us when we wake,
Ere through the world our way we take,
Till in the ocean of Thy love
We lose ourselves in heaven above.

Rev. John Keble, 1820, 1827.

BpC	84
BpN	56
BpS	36
CoA	565
CoC	64
CoR	om
CoS	68
Dis	256
Ep	336
EAs	768
LuC	523
LuS	530
MEN	102
MES	761
Mor	355
PrN	898
PrS	295
RAm	874
RUS	648
RfE	257
UBr	1165
BCh	259
Hat	11
HES	1029
HEM	42
HSP	1520
H&L	17
LWB	481
RSS	112
RLD	163

RETREAT. L. M. THOMAS HASTINGS, 1872.

1 From every stormy wind that blows,
From every swelling tide of woes,
There is a calm, a sure retreat—
'Tis found beneath the mercy-seat.

2 There is a place where Jesus sheds
The oil of gladness on our heads,
A place than all besides more sweet—
It is the blood-bought mercy-seat.

3 There is a scene, where spirits blend,
Where friend holds fellowship with friend;
Though sundered far, by faith they meet
Around one common mercy-seat.

4 There, there on eagles' wings we soar,
And sin and sense molest no more,
And heaven comes down our souls to greet,
And glory crowns the mercy-seat.

5 Oh, let my hand forget her skill,
My tongue be silent, cold and still,
This throbbing heart forget to beat,
If I forget the mercy-seat!

Rev. Hugh Stowell, 1827, 1828.

BpC 611
BpN 397
BpS 27
CoA 302
CoC 685
CoR 385
CoS 845
Dis 246
Ep 406
EAs 394
LuC om
LuS 328
MEN 684
MES 724
Mor 418
PrN 855
PrS 475
RAm 667
RUS 667
RfE 388
UBr 787

BCh 384
Hat 1055
HES 1000
HEM 518
HSP 63
H&L om
LWB 431
RSS 69
RLD 96

SHEPHERD. 8s, 7s & 4s.
WILLIAM B. BRADBURY, 1859.

1 Saviour! like a shepherd lead us;
  Much we need Thy tender care;
In Thy pleasant pastures feed us,
  For our use Thy folds prepare:
    Blessed Jesus!
Thou hast bought us; Thine we are.

2 We are Thine; do thou befriend us,
  Be the guardian of our way;
Keep Thy flock, from sin defend us,
  Seek us when we go astray:
    Blessed Jesus:
Hear young children when they pray.

3 Thou hast promised to receive us,
  Poor and sinful though we be;
Thou hast mercy to relieve us,
  Grace to cleanse, and power to free.
    Blessed Jesus!
Let us early turn to Thee.

4 Early let us seek Thy favor,
  Early let us do Thy will:
Holy Lord, our only Saviour!
  With Thy grace our bosom fill:
    Blessed Jesus!
Thou hast loved us, love us still.

Dorothy Anne Thrupp, 1838.

BpC	om
BpN	576
BpS	1028
CoA	622
CoC	526
CoR	om
CoS	400
Dis	om
Ep	229
EAs	754
LuC	om
LuS	98
MEN	872
MES	om
Mor	1413
PrN	941
PrS	om
RAm	om
RUS	295
RfE	200
UBr	om
BCh	om
Hat	1313
HES	1191
HEM	893
HSP	826
H&L	554
LWB	om
RSS	815
RLD	om

OLIVET. 6s & 4s. LOWELL MASON, 1831.

1 My faith looks up to Thee,
  Thou lamb of Calvary,
    Saviour divine!
  Now hear me while I pray,
  Take all my guilt away,
  Oh let me from this day
    Be wholly Thine.

2 May Thy rich grace impart
  Strength to my fainting heart
    My zeal inspire;
  As Thou hast died for me,
  Oh may my love to Thee
  Pure, warm and changeless be,
    A living fire.

3 While life's dark maze I tread,
  And griefs around me spread,
    Be Thou my guide;
  Bid darkness turn to day,
  Wipe sorrow's tears away,
  Nor let me ever stray
    From Thee aside.

4 When ends life's transient dream,
  When death's cold, sullen stream
    Shall o'er me roll,
  Blest Saviour, then in love
  Fear and distress remove;
  O, bear me safe above,
    A ransomed soul.

BpC 709
BpN 384
BpS 1017
CoA 364
CoC 546
CoR 308
CoS 722
Dis 658
Ep 237
EAs 391
LuC 435
LuS 364
MEN 762
MES 371
Mor 1244
PrN 335
PrS 274
RAm 449
RUS 407
RfE 202
UBr 587

BCh 139
Hat 1004
HES 728
HEM 381
HSP 1181
H&L 334
LWB 300
RSS 600
RLD 793

Rev. Ray Palmer, 1830, 1831.

151

PASSION CHORALE. 7s, 6s. D. H. L. HASSLER, († 1612.)

7s, 6s. Double.

1 O sacred Head, now wounded!
    With grief and shame weighed down;
  Now scornfully surrounded
    With thorns, Thine only crown!
  O sacred Head! what glory,
    What bliss till now was Thine!
  Now all despised and gory,
    I joy to call Thee mine.

2 On me, as Thou art dying,
    Oh, turn Thy pitying eye!
  To Thee for mercy crying,
    Before Thy cross I lie.
  Thine, Thine the bitter passion,
    Thy pain is all for me;
  Mine, mine the deep transgression,
    My sins are all on Thee.

3 The joy can ne'er be spoken,
    Above all joys beside,
  When in Thy body broken
    I thus with safety hide.
  My Lord of life, desiring
    Thy glory now to see,
  Beside the cross expiring,
    I'd breathe my soul to Thee.

4 What language shall I borrow
    To thank Thee, dearest Friend,
  For all this dying sorrow,
    Of all my woes the end?
  Oh, can I leave Thee ever?
    Then do not Thou leave me:
  Lord, let me never, never
    Outlive my love to Thee.

5 Be near when I am dying;
    Then close beside me stand;
  Let me, while faint and sighing,
    Lean calmly on Thy hand:
  These eyes new faith receiving,
    From Thine eye shall not move;
  For he who dies believing,
    Dies safely in Thy love.

                St. Bernard of Clairvaux, xii Cent.
Rev. Paul Gerhart, 1659. Rev. James Waddell Alexander, 1830, 1849.

REST. L. M.   WM. B. BRADBURY, 1844.

1 Asleep in Jesus! blessed sleep!
   From which none ever wake to weep;
   A calm and undisturbed repose,
   Unbroken by the last of foes.

2 Asleep in Jesus! oh, how sweet
   To be for such a slumber meet!
   With holy confidence to sing
   That death has lost its venomed sting.

3 Asleep in Jesus! peaceful rest!
   Whose waking is supremely blest;
   No fear—no woe, shall dim the hour
   That manifests the Saviour's power.

4 Asleep in Jesus! oh, for me
   May such a blissful refuge be:
   Securely shall my ashes lie,
   Waiting the summons from on high.

5 Asleep in Jesus! time nor space
   Debars this precious hiding-place:
   On Indian plains, or Lapland snows,
   Believers find the same repose.

6 Asleep in Jesus! far from thee
   Thy kindred and their graves may be;
   But thine is still a blessed sleep,
   From which none ever wake to weep.

                Mrs. Margaret Mackay, 1832.

BpC	986
BpN	639
BpS	1100
CoA	509
CoC	828
CoR	601
CoS	1195
Dis	263
Ep	260
EAs	797
LuC	555
LuS	560
MEN	979
MES	575
Mor	411
PrN	735
PrS	650
RAm	948
RUS	574
RfE	218
UBr	1077
BCh	564
Hat	1362
HES	1292
HEM	680
HSP	704
H&L	455
LWB	518
RSS	944
RLD	1096

GOD SAVE THE KING. 6s & 4s.
HENRY CARY, († 1743.)

1 God bless our native land!
  Firm may she ever stand,
    Through storm and night:
  When the wild tempests rave,
  Ruler of wind and wave,
  Do Thou our country save
    By Thy great might!

2 For her our prayer shall rise
  To God, above the skies;
    On Him we wait:
  Thou who art ever nigh,
  Guarding with watchful eye,
  To Thee aloud we cry,
    God save the State!

Rev. Charles T. Brooks, 1835.
Rev. John Sullivan Dwight, 1844.

BpC 935
BpN 692
BpS 1256
CoA 592
CoC 951
CoR om
CoS 1111
Dis 599
Ep 309
EAs 739
LuC 493
LuS 539
MEN 1090
MES om
Mor 1232
PrN 830
PrS om
RAm 899
RUS 603
RfE 236
UBr 1227

BCh 540
Hat 1299
HES 1166
HEM 745
HSP 1177
H&L om
LWB 467
RSS om
RLD om

WOODWORTH. L. M.
WM. B. BRADBURY, 1849.

1 Just as I am, without one plea
   But that Thy blood was shed for me,
   And that Thou bidst me come to Thee,
     O Lamb of God, I come!

2 Just as I am, and waiting not
   To rid my soul of one dark blot,
   To Thee, Whose blood can cleanse each spot,
     O Lamb of God, I come!

3 Just as I am, though tossed about
   With many a conflict, many a doubt,
   Fightings and fears within, without,
     O Lamb of God, I come!

4 Just as I am, poor, wretched, blind,
   Sight, riches, healing of the mind,
   Yea, all I need in Thee to find,
     O Lamb of God, I come!

5 Just as I am; Thou wilt receive,
   Wilt welcome, pardon, cleanse, relieve;
   Because Thy promise I believe,
     O Lamb of God, I come!

6 Just as I am; Thy love unknown
   Has broken every barrier down:
   Now to be Thine, yea, Thine alone,
     O Lamb of God, I come!

                Miss Charlotte Elliott, 1836.

BpC	487
BpN	283
BpS	656
CoA	345
CoC	333
CoR	274
CoS	559
Dis	612
Ep	392
EAs	255
LuC	366
LuS	311
MEN	393
MES	332
Mor	1144
PrN	192
PrS	218
RAm	425
RUS	166
RfE	457
UBr	498
BCh	350
Hat	070
HES	496
HEM	330
HSP	26
H&L	172
LWB	286
RSS	457
RLD	609

BETHANY. 6s & 4s.

LOWELL MASON, 1859.

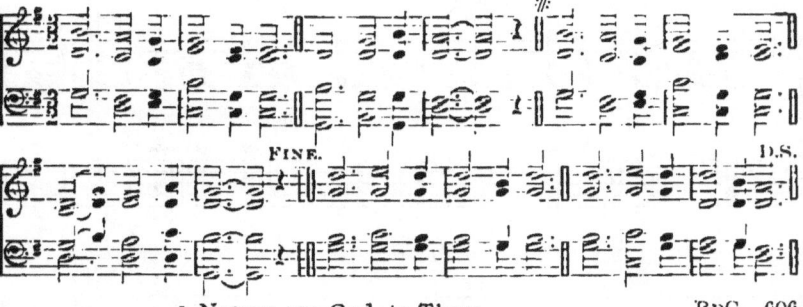

Used by arrangement with Oliver Ditson Company, owners of the Copyright

1 Nearer, my God, to Thee;
    Nearer to Thee!
  E'en though it be a cross
    That raiseth me,
  Still all my song shall be,
  Nearer, my God, to Thee,
    Nearer to Thee!

2 Though like the wanderer,
    The sun gone down,
  Darkness be over me,
    My rest a stone,—
  Yet in my dreams I'd be
  Nearer, my God, to Thee,
    Nearer to Thee!

3 There let the way appear
    Steps unto heaven;
  All that Thou sendest me
    In mercy given;
  Angels to beckon me
  Nearer, my God, to Thee,
    Nearer to Thee!

4 Then with my waking thoughts
    Bright with Thy praise,
  Out of my stony griefs
    Bethel I'll raise,—
  So by my woes to be
  Nearer, my God, to Thee,
    Nearer to Thee!

5 Or if on joyful wing
    Cleaving the sky,
  Sun, moon and stars forgot,
    Upward I fly,
  Still all my song shall be
  Nearer, my God, to Thee,
    Nearer to Thee!

Mrs. Sarah Flower Adams, 1841.

BpC 606
BpN 387
BpS 946
CoA 435
CoC 555
CoR 311
CoS 989
Dis 689
Ep 507
EAs 423
LuC 536
LuS 393
MEN 724
MES 495
Mor 1241
PrN 474
PrS 320
RAm 589
RUS 214
RfE 458
UBr 709

BCh 419
Hat 911
HES 734
HEM 480
HSP 1223
H&L 347
LWB 358
RSS 485
RLD 680

ZEBULON. H. M.

LOWELL MASON, 1830.

1 One sole baptismal sign,
  One Lord, below, above,
One faith, one hope divine,
  One only watchword—Love:
From different temples though it rise,
One song ascendeth to the skies.

2 Our sacrifice is one;
  One Priest before the throne:
The slain, the risen Son,
  Redeemer, Lord alone!
And sighs from contrite hearts that spring,
Our chief, our choicest offering.

3 Oh may that holy prayer,
  His tenderest and His last,
His constant, latest care
  Ere to His throne He passed,
No longer unfulfilled remain,
The world's offence, His people's stain!

4 Head of thy church beneath!
  The catholic, the true,
On all her members breathe;
  Her broken frame renew!
Then shall Thy perfect will be done
When Christians love and live as one.

George Robinson, 1842.

BpC 796
BpN om
BpS om
CoA om
CoC om
CoR om
CoS 872
Dis 153
Ep 197
EAs om
LuC 277
LuS om
MEN 800
MES om
Mor 1187
PrN 592
PrS om
RAm 769
RUS om
RfE om
UBr om

BCh 403
Hat om
HES 829
HEM om
HSP om
H&L 428
LWB om
RSS 752
RLD 927

ATHENS. C. M.   FELICE GIARDINI, 1760.

1 I heard the voice of Jesus say,
  "Come unto Me and rest;
Lay down, thou weary one, lay down
  Thy head upon My breast."
I came to Jesus as I was,
  Weary, and worn, and sad;
I found in Him a resting-place,
  And He has made me glad.

2 I heard the voice of Jesus say,
  "Behold I freely give
The living water; thirsty one,
  Stoop down, and drink, and live."
I came to Jesus and I drank
  Of that life-giving stream;
My thirst was quenched, my soul revived,
  And now I live in Him.

3 I heard the voice of Jesus say,
  "I am this dark world's light;
Look unto Me, thy morn shall rise,
  And all thy day be bright."
I looked to Jesus, and I found
  In Him my star, my sun;
And in that light of life I'll walk
  Till travelling days are done.

        Rev. Horatius Bonar, 1846.

BpC	511
BpN	487
BpS	870
CoA	367
CoC	346
CoR	277
CoS	565
Dis	om
Ep	528
EAs	452
LuC	106
LuS	320
MEN	426
MES	om
Mor	1464
PrN	255
PrS	273
RAm	388
RUS	731
RfE	346
UBr	666
BCh	152
Hat	679
HES	599
HEM	339
HSP	om
H&L	276
LWB	273
RSS	633
RLD	357

CALVARY. 8s & 7s. D.
S. STANLEY, († 1822.)

1. A few more years shall roll
   A few more seasons come;
   And we shall be with those that rest,
   Asleep within the tomb.
   Then, O my Lord, prepare
   My soul for that great day;
   O wash me in Thy precious blood,
   And take my sins away.

2. A few more suns shall set
   O'er these dark hills of time;
   And we shall be where suns are not,
   A far serener clime.
   Then, O my Lord, prepare
   My soul for that blest day;
   O wash me in Thy precious blood,
   And take my sins away.

BpC 984
BpN 631
BpS 1131
CoA 602
CoC 604
CoR 572
CoS 1220
Dis 454
Ep 28
EAs 796
LuC 541
LuS 586
MEN 957
MES om
Mor 1490
PrN 756
PrS 415
RAm 937
RUS 19
RfE 31
UBr 1089

BCh 614
Hat 1373
HES 1206
HEM 678
HSP 580
H&L 417
LWB 495
RSS 948
RLD 1099

8s & 7s. Double.

3 A few more storms shall beat
   On this wild, rocky shore;
  And we shall be where tempests cease,
   And surges swell no more.
  Then, O my Lord, prepare
   My soul for that calm day;
  O wash me in Thy precious blood,
   And take my sins away.

4 A few more struggles here,
   A few more partings o'er,
  A few more toils, a few more tears,
   And we shall weep no more.
  Then, O my Lord, prepare
   My soul for that blest day;
  O wash me in Thy precious blood,
   And take my sins away.

5 A few more Sabbaths here
   Shall cheer us on our way;
  And we shall reach the endless rest,
   The eternal Sabbath-day.
  Then, O my Lord, prepare
   My soul for that sweet day;
  O wash me in Thy precious blood,
   And take my sins away.

6 'Tis but a little while
   And He shall come again,
  Who died that we might live, Who lives
   That we with Him may reign.
  Then, O my Lord, prepare
   My soul for that glad day;
  O wash me in Thy precious blood,
   And take my sins away.

                    Rev. Dr. Horatius Bonar, 1842, 1844.

GREENWOOD. S. M.
JOSEPH E. SWEETZER, 1849.

1 It is not death to die—
  To leave this weary road,
And, 'midst the brotherhood on high
  To be at home with God.

2 It is not death to close
  The eye long dimmed by tears,
And wake, in glorious repose
  To spend eternal years.

3 It is not death to bear
  The wrench that sets us free
From dungeon chain,—to breathe the air
  Of boundless liberty.

4 It is not death to fling
  Aside this sinful dust,
And rise, on strong, exulting wing,
  To live among the just.

5 Jesus, Thou Prince of life !
  Thy chosen cannot die ;
Like Thee, they conquer in the strife,
  To reign with Thee on high.

Rev. Cesar Malan, 1832.
Rev. Geo. W. Bethune, (tr.) 1847.

BpC	985
BpN	632
BpS	1130
CoA	505
CoC	om
CoR	588
CoS	1178
Dis	om
Ep	97
EAs	813
LuC	om
LuS	466
MEN	993
MES	601
Mor	1299
PrN	755
PrS	833
RAm	940
RUS	577
RfE	om
UBr	1088
RCh	567
Hat	1374
HES	1332
HEM	om
HSP	om
H&L	om
LWB	om
RSS	961
RLD	1100

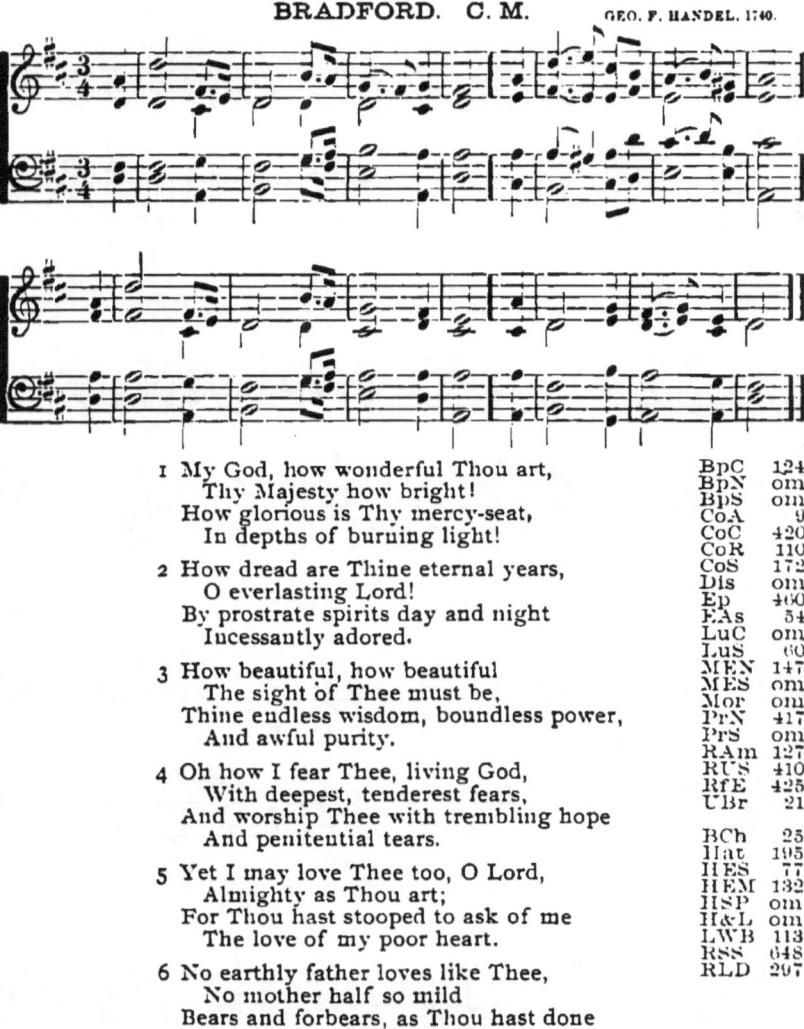

BRADFORD. C. M.   GEO. F. HANDEL. 1740.

1 My God, how wonderful Thou art,
   Thy Majesty how bright!
  How glorious is Thy mercy-seat,
   In depths of burning light!

2 How dread are Thine eternal years,
   O everlasting Lord!
  By prostrate spirits day and night
   Incessantly adored.

3 How beautiful, how beautiful
   The sight of Thee must be,
  Thine endless wisdom, boundless power,
   And awful purity.

4 Oh how I fear Thee, living God,
   With deepest, tenderest fears,
  And worship Thee with trembling hope
   And penitential tears.

5 Yet I may love Thee too, O Lord,
   Almighty as Thou art;
  For Thou hast stooped to ask of me
   The love of my poor heart.

6 No earthly father loves like Thee,
   No mother half so mild
  Bears and forbears, as Thou hast done
   With me, Thy sinful child.

7 My God, how wonderful Thou art,
   Thou everlasting Friend!
  On Thee I stay my trusting heart,
   Till faith in vision end.

              Rev. Frederic W. Faber, 1848.

BpC	124
BpN	om
BpS	om
CoA	9
CoC	420
CoR	110
CoS	172
Dis	om
Ep	400
FAs	54
LuC	om
LuS	60
MEN	147
MES	om
Mor	om
PrN	417
PrS	om
RAm	127
RUS	410
RfE	425
UBr	21
BCh	25
Hat	195
HES	77
HEM	132
HSP	om
H&L	om
LWB	113
RSS	648
RLD	207

ST. JUDE. 6s. D.
CARL MARIA von WEBER.

6s. Double.

1 Thy way, not mine, O Lord,
    However dark it be!
Lead me by Thine own hand;
    Choose out the path for me.
I dare not choose my lot:
    I would not, if I might;
Choose Thou for me, my God,
    So shall I walk aright.

2 The kingdom that I seek
    Is Thine: so let the way
That leads to it be Thine,
    Else I must surely stray.
Take Thou my cup, and it
    With joy or sorrow fill,
As best to Thee may seem;
    Choose Thou my good and ill.

3 Choose Thou for me my friends,
    My sickness or my health;
Choose Thou my cares for me,
    My poverty or wealth.
Not mine, not mine the choice,
    In things or great or small;
Be Thou my guide, my strength,
    My wisdom, and my all.

        Rev. Horatio Bonar, D. D., 1857.

BpC	651
BpN	431
BpS	om
CoA	434
CoC	541
CoR	438
CoS	928
Dis	om
Ep	254
EAs	523
LuC	om
LuS	347
MEN	655
MES	om
Mor	473
PrN	313
PrS	29
RAm	615
RUS	192
RfE	420
UBr	865
BCh	453
Hat	1007
HES	770
HEM	507
HSP	om
H&L	324
LWB	371
RSS	727
RLD	874

WESTMINSTER.   JAMES TURLE, 1858.

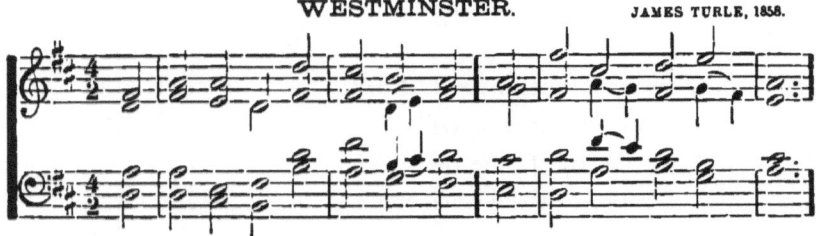

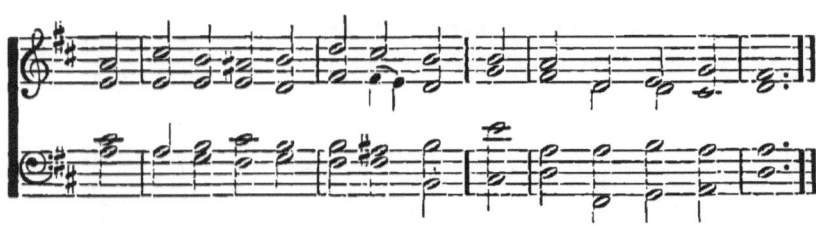

1 My God, accept my heart this day,
    And make it always Thine,
  That I from Thee no more may stray,
    No more from Thee decline.

2 Before the cross of Him who died,
    Behold, I prostrate fall;
  Let every sin be crucified,
    And Christ be all in all.

3 Anoint me with Thy heavenly grace,
    And seal me for Thine own;
  That I may see Thy glorious face,
    And worship near Thy throne.

4 May the dear blood, once shed for me,
    My blest atonement prove,
  That I, from first to last, may be
    The purchase of Thy love.

5 Let every thought and work and word,
    To Thee be ever given;
  Then life shall be Thy service, Lord,
    And death the gate of heaven.

         M. Bridges, 1848.

BpC om
BpN om
BpS 719
CoA om
CoC 849
CoR om
CoS om
Dis om
Ep 234
EAs 343
LuC 325
LuS 412
MEN 468
MES om
Mor 135
PrN 687
PrS 766
RAm 479
RUS 502
RfE om
UBr 646

BCh om
Hat 685
HES om
HEM om
HSP om
IL&L 313
LWB om
RSS om
RLD om

HEBER. C. M.
GEORGE KINGSLEY, 1838.

1 Jesus, the very thought of Thee
　With sweetness fills my breast:
　But sweeter far Thy face to see,
　　And in Thy presence rest.

2 Nor voice can sing, nor heart can frame,
　Nor can the memory find
　A sweeter sound than Thy blest name,
　　O Saviour of mankind!

3 O hope of every contrite heart!
　O joy of all the meek!
　To those who fall how kind Thou art!
　　How good to those who seek!

4 But what to those who find? Ah! this
　Nor pen nor tongue can show;
　The love of Jesus, what it is,
　　None but His loved ones know.

5 Jesus, our only joy be Thou,
　As Thou our prize wilt be;
　Jesus, be Thou our glory now,
　　And through eternity.

　　　Bernard of Clairvaux, 1130.
　　　Rev. Edward Caswall, 1849.

BpC 539
BpN 348
BpS 468
CoA 494
CoC 486
CoR 233
CoS 687
Dis om
Ep 455
EAs 449
LuC 244
LuS 176
MEN 700
MES 140
Mor 205
PrN 232
PrS 305
RAm 526
RUS 365
RfE 426
UBr 548

BCh 155
Hat 731
HES 564
HEM 361
HSP om
H&L 151
LWB 152
RSS 614
RLD 773

EWING or JENNER. 7s & 6s. D.

Capt. ALEX. EWING, 1860.

7s & 6s. Double.

1 Jerusalem the golden!
    With milk and honey blest,
  Beneath thy contemplation
    Sink heart and voice opprest:
  I know not, O I know not
    What joys await us there,
  What radiancy of glory,
    What bliss beyond compare.

2 They stand, those halls of Sion,
    All jubilant with song,
  And bright with many an angel,
    And all the martyr throng;
  The Prince is ever with them,
    The daylight is serene;
  The pastures of the blessed
    Are decked in glorious sheen.

3 There is the throne of David;
    And there, from care released,
  The song of them that triumph,
    The shout of them that feast;
  And they, who with their Leader
    Have conquered in the fight,
  Forever and forever
    Are clad in robes of white.

4 O sweet and blessèd country,
    The home of God's elect!
  O sweet and blessèd country,
    That eager hearts expect!
  Jesus in mercy bring us
    To that dear land of rest;
  Who art, with God the Father,
    And Spirit, ever blest.

Bernard of Clugny, xii Cent.
Rev. John Mason Neale, 1851, 1858.

ST. HILDA. 7s & 6s. D. J. H. KNECHT and E. HUSBAND.

7s & 6s. Double.

1 Brief life is here our portion,
    Brief sorrow, short-lived care;
  The life that knows no ending,
    The tearless life is there:
  O happy retribution!
    Short toil, eternal rest—
  For mortals and for sinners
    A mansion with the blest.

2 And now we fight the battle,
    But then shall wear the crown
  Of full and everlasting
    And passionless renown;
  And He Whom now we trust in
    Shall then be seen and known,
  And they that know and see Him
    Shall have Him for their own.

3 The morning shall awaken,
    The shadows shall decay,
  And each true-hearted servant
    Shall shine as doth the day:
  There God, our King and portion,
    In fullness of His grace,
  Shall we behold forever,
    And worship face to face.

4 O sweet and blessèd country,
    The home of God's elect,
  O sweet and blessèd country
    That eager hearts expect!
  Jesus, in mercy bring us
    To that dear land of rest;
  Who art, with God the Father,
    And Spirit, ever blest.

Bernard of Clugny, c. 1145.
Rev. John Mason Neale, tr., 1851.

ST. GEORGE. C. M.   HENRY J. GAUNTLETT.

1 We give Thee but Thine own,
   Whate'er the gift may be:
 All that we have is Thine alone,
   A trust, O Lord, from Thee.

2 May we Thy bounties thus
   As stewards true receive,
 And gladly, as Thou blessest us,
   To Thee our first-fruits give.

3 O, hearts are bruised and dead,
   And homes are bare and cold,
 And lambs, for whom the Shepherd bled,
   Are straying from the fold.

4 To comfort and to bless,
   To find a balm for woe,
 To tend the lone and fatherless,
   Is angels' work below.

5 The captive to release,
   To God the lost to bring,
 To teach the way of life and peace,
   It is a Christ-like thing.

6 And we believe Thy word,
   Though dim our faith may be;
 Whate'er for Thine we do, O Lord,
   We do it unto Thee.

                              Bp. W. W. How, (1858,) 1864.

BpC	om
BpN	451
BpS	929
CoA	267
CoC	om
CoR	457
CoS	om
Dis	om
Ep	299
EAs	540
LuC	777
LuS	om
MEN	982
MES	892
Mor	1361
PrN	276
PrS	om
RAm	50
RUS	361
RfE	295
UBr	821
BCh	om
Hat	1264
HES	1055
HEM	533
HSP	om
H&L	481
LWB	om
RSS	780
RLD	902

DIX (ORISONS). 7s.
CONRAD KOCHER, 1838.

1 As with gladness men of old
Did the guiding star behold;
As with joy they hailed its light,
Leading onward, beaming bright;
So, most gracious Lord, may we
Evermore be led to Thee.

2 As with joyful steps they sped
To that lowly manger-bed,
There to bend the knee before
Him whom heaven and earth adore,
So may we with willing feet
Ever seek Thy mercy-seat.

3 As they offered gifts most rare
At that manger rude and bare;
So may we with holy joy,
Pure and free from sin's alloy,
All our costliest treasures bring,
Christ! to Thee, our heavenly King.

4 Holy Jesus, every day
Keep us in the narrow way;
And, when earthly things are past,
Bring our ransomed souls at last
Where they need no star to guide,
Where no clouds Thy glory hide.

William Chatterton Dix, 1861.

BpC	223
BpN	104
BpS	om
CoA	54
CoC	168
CoR	302
CoS	om
Dis	om
Ep	45
EAs	om
LuC	140
LuS	om
MEN	182
MES	om
Mor	1259
PrN	115
PrS	712
RAm	183
RUS	100
RfE	41
UBr	om
BCh	om
Hat	797
HES	797
HEM	171
HSP	om
H&L	206
LWB	om
RSS	63
RLD	311

EIN' FESTE BURG.

MARTIN LUTHER, 1529.

EIN' FESTE BURG. Concluded.

1 A mighty fortress is our God,
   A bulwark never failing;
  Our helper He amid the flood
    Of mortal ill prevailing.
      For still our ancient foe
      Doth seek to work us woe;
      His craft and power are great;
      And, armed with cruel hate,
  On earth is not his equal..

2 Did we in our own strength confide,
   Our striving would be losing;
  Were not the right man on our side,—
    The man of God's own choosing.
      Dost ask who that may be?
      Christ Jesus: it is He;
      Lord Sabaoth His name,
      From age to age the same,
  And He must win the battle.

3 And though this world, with devils filled,
   Should threaten to undo us,
  We will not fear; for God hath willed
    His truth to triumph through us.
      The Prince of Darkness grim,—
      We tremble not for him;
      His rage we can endure,
      For, lo! his doom is sure;
  One little word shall fell him.

4 That word above all earthly powers—
   No thanks to them—abideth;
  The Spirit and the gifts are ours,
    Through Him who with us sideth.
      Let goods and kindred go,
      This mortal life also;
      The body they may kill,
      God's truth abideth still;
  His kingdom is forever.

          Dr. Martin Luther, 1529.
          Dr. F. H. Hedge, tr., 1852.

BpC	om
BpN	94
BpS	om
CoA	203
CoC	392
CoR	134
CoS	om
Dis	om
Ep	397
EAs	79
LuC	274
LuS	p 16
MEN	166
MES	om
Mor	1028
PrN	953
PrS	om
RAm	698
RUS	1578
RfE	369
UBr	om
BCh	om
Hat	546
HES	842
HEM	435
HSP	om
H&L	467
LWB	om
RSS	215
RLD	930

AURELIA. 7s, 6s. D. Samuel Sebastian Wesley, 1864.

7s, 6s. Double.

1 O day of rest and gladness,
    O day of joy and light,
O balm of care and sadness,
    Most beautiful, most bright;
On thee, the high and lowly,
    Bending before the throne,
Sing, Holy, Holy, Holy,
    To the great Three in One.

2 On thee, at the creation,
    The light first had its birth;
On thee, for our salvation
    Christ rose from depths of earth;
On thee, our Lord, victorious,
    The Spirit sent from Heaven,
And thus on thee, most glorious,
    A triple light was given.

3 To-day on weary nations
    The heavenly manna falls;
To holy convocations
    The silver trumpet calls,
Where gospel light is glowing
    With pure and radiant beams,
And living water flowing
    With soul-refreshing streams.

4 New graces ever gaining
    From this our day of rest,
We reach the rest remaining
    To spirits of the blest:
To Holy Ghost be praises,
    To Father and to Son;
The Church her voice upraises
    To thee, blest Three in One.

Bp. Chr. Wordsworth, 1862.

INDEX OF SUBJECTS.

Ascension, 44, 135.
Brotherly love, 83, 158, 172.
Children, 118, 144, 150.
Christ's advent, 62.
    birth, 39, 49, 119, 120, 123, 173.
    death, 17, 68, 84, 100, 127, 153.
    resurrection, 40.
    ascension, 44.
    exaltation, 73, 101, 135.
    universal reign, 31, 80, 117, 123, 130, 142.
    love, 53, 93, 144, 146, 148, 150, 167.
    second advent, 56, 60, 96, 113, 161.
Christian pilgrimage, 39, 59, 65, 79, 104, 134, 138.
    consecration, 63, 67, 166.
    conflict, 54, 97, 114, 127, 171, 175.
    responsibility, 53, 66, 97.
    perseverance, 103.
    fellowship, 83, 58, 172.
Christmas, 34, 49, 119, 120, 123, 173.
Church, 95, 106.
Church triumphant, 2, 52, 127, 143, 169, 171.
Close of worship, 82.
Communion, 133.
Communion of saints, 57.
Contentment, 1, 4, 75, 165.
Conversion, 26, 45, 70, 86, 137, 147, 156, 166.
Courage, 7, 10, 11, 33, 54, 59, 65, 97.
Crucifixion, 17, 68, 84, 100, 127, 153.
Death, 154, 162.
Deliverance, 3.

Easter, 40.
Evening, 6, 140, 145, 148.
Faith, 3, 19, 23, 151.
Fruition of God, 4.
God's creative power, 21, 34, 109.
    love, 85, 157, 163.
    providence, 88.
    watchfulness, 23, 24, 27, 95, 103, 104, 108, 165, 175.
Good news, 11.
Harvest, 81.
Holy Spirit, 15, 70, 121, 129.
Heaven, 1, 2, 10, 12, 57, 60, 127, 134, 143, 160, 169.
Joy, 8, 28, 59, 93.
Ministry, 11, 47.
Missions, 31, 80, 117, 125, 129–132.
Morning, 5, 16, 41, 115.
National, 81, 107, 155.
New Year, 27, 91, 160.
Pentecost, 121.
Praise, 9, 24, 30, 32, 34, 61, 69, 99, 126.
Prayer, 89, 92, 122, 149.
Redemption, 14, 37, 39, 43, 45, 51, 62, 64, 111, 159.
Regeneration, 51, 53.
Sabbath, 18, 25, 29, 35, 92, 110, 177.
Sanctification, 46, 48.
Scriptures, 74.
Second coming, 56, 60, 96, 113, 161.
Temptation, 71, 127, 140.
Thanksgiving, 81.
Trials, 36, 43, 105, 108, 138, 139, 161.
Trinity, 55, 111, 141.

INDEX OF AUTHORS.

Adams, Sarah Flower (1805-1848), 157.
Addison, Joseph (1672-1719), 19, 21, 23.
Alexander, James W. (1804-1859), 153.
Allen, James (1734-1804), 68.
Baker, Francis (XVI century), 2.
Bakewell, John (1721-1819), 73.
Barbauld, Anna Lætitia (1743-1825), 81.
Baxter, Richard (1615-1691), 1.
Bernard of Clairvaux (1091-1153), 153, 167.
Bernard of Clugny (c. 1145), 169, 171.
Bethune, Geo. W. (1805-1862), 162.
Bonar, Horatius (1808-1889), 159, 160, 165.
Bowring, Sir John (1792-1872), 142.
Brady, Nicholas (1659-1726), 3, 4.
Bridges, Matthew (b. 1800———), 166.
Brooks, Charles Timothy (1813-1883), 155.
Bruce, Michael (1746-1767), 63.
Burdsall, Richard (1735-1824), 137.
Caswall, Edward (1814-1878), 167.
Cawood, John (1775-1852), 120.
Cennick, John (1718-1755), 56, 59.
Collyer, William Bengo (1782-1854), 113.
Cooper, E. (XIX century), 111.
Cotterill, Thomas (1779-1823), 105, 110, 113.
Cowper, William (1731-1800), 85-88.
Dix, Wm. Chatterton (b. 1837), 173.
Doane, Geo. W. (1799-1859), 145, 146.
Doddridge, Philip (1702-1751), 62-67.
Dwight, John S. (b. 1812), 155.
Dwight, Timothy (1752-1817), 106.
Elliott, Charlotte (1789-1871), 156.
Evans, Jonathan (1749-1809), 100.
F., C. (1804), 107.
Faber, Frederic W. (1814-1863), 163.
Fawcett, John (1739-1817), 82, 83.
Francis, Benjamin (1734-1799), 78.
Gerhardt, Paul (1607-1676), 153.
Grant, Sir Robert (1785-1838), 108, 109.
Grigg, Joseph (1722-1768), 78.
Hammond, William (1719-1783), 61.
Hart, Joseph (1712-1768), 70.
Haweis, Thomas (1732-1820), 105.
Heath, George (XVIII century), 97.
Heber, Reginald (1783-1826), 117-119.
Hedge, Frederic Henry (1805-1890), 175.
How, William Walsham (b. 1823), 172.
Keble, John (1792-1866), 148.
Keith, George (XVIII century), 103.

INDEX OF AUTHORS.

Kelly, Thomas (1769-1854), 135.
Ken, Thomas (1637-1711), 5, 6.
Luther, Martin (1483-1546), 175.
Lyte, Henry Francis (1793-1847), 138-140.
Mackay, Margaret (1802-1887), 154.
Madan, Martin (1726-1790), 39, 56.
Malan, Henri Abraham César (1787-1864), 162.
Marriott, John (1780-1825), 141.
Medley, Samuel (1738-1799), 101.
Montgomery, James (1771-1854), 121-134.
Muhlenberg, Wm. Augustus (1796-1877), 143, 144.
Neale, John Mason (1818-1866), 169, 171.
Newton, John (1725-1807), 89-93, 95, 96.
Ollivers, Thomas (1725-1799), 77.
Onderdonk, Henry Ustick (1789-1858), 147.
Palmer, Ray (1808-18—), 151.
Perronet, Edward (1726-1792), 99.
Rippon, John (1751-1836), 99.
Robinson, George (1842-——), 158.
Robinson, Robert (1735-1790), 69.
Scott, Elizabeth (1708-1776), 110.
Seagrave, Robert (1693-——), 60.
Shirley, Walter (1725-1786), 68.
Shrubsole, William (1759-1829), 115.
Steele, Anne (1716-1778), 71, 74, 75.
Stennett, Joseph (1663-1713), 35.
Stowell, Hugh (1799-1865), 149.
Tate, Nahum (———-——), 3, 4.
Thrupp, Dorothy Anne (1779-1847), 150.
Toplady, Augustus M. (1740-1778), 84.
Watts, Isaac (1674-1748), 7-18, 24-34.
Wesley, Charles (1707-1788), 34, 39-41, 43-49, 51, 53-55, 57, 58.
Wesley, John (1703-1791), 36, 37.
White, Henry Kirke (1785-1806), 114.
Williams, Helen Maria (1762-1827), 104.
Williams, William (1717-1791), 79, 80.
Wordsworth, Christopher (1807-1885), 177.
Zinzendorf, Nicolaus Ludwig von (1700-1760), 36, 37.

INDEX OF TUNES.

Amsterdam	7s and 6s	*J. Nares*	60
Antioch	C. M.	*Handel-Mason*	28
Ariel	C. P. M.	*L. Mason*	101
Arlington	C. M.	*Thos. A. Arne*	33
Athens	C. M.	*F. Giardini*	159
Aurelia	7s and 6s, D.	*S. S. Wesley*	176
Austria	8s and 7s, D.	*Jos. Haydn*	94
Autumn	8s and 7s, D.	*Spanish*	72
Avon	C. M.	*H. Wilson*	133
Balerma	C. M.	*Spanish*	87
Barby	C. M.	*Wm. Tansur*	4
Benevento	7s, D.	*S. Webbe*	91
Bethany	6s and 4s	*L. Mason*	157
Beulah	7s, D.	*E. Ives, Jr.*	127
Boylston	S. M.	*L. Mason*	83
Bradford	C. M.	*Handel*	163
Brattle Street	C. M. D.	*Ig. Pleyel*	104
Brest	8s, 7s and 4s	*L. Mason*	96
Brown	C. M.	*W. B. Bradbury*	57
Brownell	L. M. 6l.	*Jos. Haydn*	19
Byefield	C. M.	*T. Hastings*	122
Calvary	8s and 7s, D.	*S. Stanley*	160
Cambridge	C. M.	*J. Randall*	14
Carlisle	S. M.	*Ch. Lockhart*	66
Chesterfield	C. M.	*T. Haweis*	62
Chimes	C. M.	*L. Mason*	74
Christmas	C. M.	*Handel*	65
Consummatum est	8s, 7s and 4s	*J. Stanley*	100
Coronation	C. M.	*O. Holden*	98
Coventry	C. M.	*S. Howard*	146
Cowper	C. M.	*L. Mason*	86
Creation	L. M. D.	*Jos. Haydn*	20, 21
Darley	L. M.	*W. H. Darley*	25
Darwell	H. M.	*J. Darwell*	29

INDEX OF TUNES.

Dennis	S. M.	H. G. Nageli	124
Dix (or Orisons)	7s, 6l.	C. Kocher	173
Doncaster	L. M.	E. Miller	67
Dorrnance	8s and 7s	I. B. Woodbury	68
Downs	C. M.	L. Mason	88
Dresden (1)	L. M.	German	107
Dresden (2)	L. M. 6l.	A. Williams	115
Duke Street	L. M.	Hatton or Reeve	30
Dundee	C. M.	Scotch Psalter, 1615	27
Easter Hymn	7s	W. H. Monk	40
Ein' Feste Burg	8s, 7s and 6s	M. Luther	174
Elizabethtown	C. M.	G. Kingsley	71
Ellesdie	8s and 7s, D.	Mozart	138
El Paran	L. M.	Carmina Sacra	35
Eltham	7s, D.	L. Mason	125
Evan	C. M.	W. H. Havergal	46
Eventide	10s	W. H. Monk	140
Ewing, or Jenner	7s and 6s, D.	A. Ewing	168
Faben	8s and 7s, D.	J. H. Wilcox	50, 51
Faith	C. M.	S. P. Tuckerman	105
Federal Street	L. M.	H. K. Oliver	78
Ferguson	S. M.	G. Kingsley	61
Fiat Lux	6s and 4s	J. B. Dykes	141
Folsom	11s and 10s	Mozart	119
Frederick	11s	G. Kingsley	143
Geneva	C. M.	J. Cole	22
Gethsemane	7s, 6l.	R. Redhead	128
God Save the King	6s and 4s	H. Cary	155
Grace Church	L. M.	Ig. Pleyel	111
Gratitude	L. M.	Bost-Hastings	16
Greenville	8s and 7s, D.	J. J. Rousseau	82
Greenwood	S. M.	J. E. Sweetzer	162
Hamburg	L. M.	L. Mason	17
Harwell	8s and 7s	L. Mason	49
Haydn	S. M.	Jos. Haydn	70
Heber	C. M.	G. Kingsley	89, 167
Holley	7s	G. Hews	145
Horton	7s	X. S. von Wartensee	90
Hursley	L. M.	Jos. Haydn	148
Italian Hymn	6s and 4s	F. Giardini	55
Jerusalem	C. M. D.	Modern Harp	2

INDEX OF TUNES. 183

Tune	Meter	Composer	Page
Judgment Hymn	P. M.	*Jos. Klug*	112, 113
Kentucky	S. M.	*A. Chapin*	58
Laban	S. M.	*L. Mason*	97
Lebanon	S. M. D.	*J. Zundel*	48
Leighton	S. M.	*H. W. Greatorex*	24
Leoni	6s, 6s, 8s and 4s	*Leoni*	76
Lisbon	S. M.	*D. Read*	18, 132
Lischer	H. M.	*L. Mason*	110
Louvan	L. M.	*V. C. Taylor*	37
Love Divine	8s and 7s, D.	*J. Zundel*	52
Luther	S. M.	*T. Hastings*	47
Lyons	10s.	*Jos. Hadyn*	109
Manoah	C. M.	*Rossini*	63
Marlow	C. M.	*L. Mason*	12
Martyn	7s, D.	*S. B. Marsh*	42
Melcombe	L. M.	*S. Webbe*	129
Mendelssohn	7s, D.	*Mendelssohn*	38
Migdol	L. M.	*L. Mason*	7
Missionary Chant	L. M.	*C. Zeuner*	31
Missionary Hymn	7s and 6s, D.	*L. Mason*	116
Morning Hymn	L. M.	*Wm. Boyce*	5
Morning Star	7s, D.	*L. Mason*	142
Naomi	C. M.	*L. Mason*	75
Nettleton	8s and 7s	*A. Nettleton*	69
Newcourt	L. P. M.	*H. Bond*	32
Nuremberg	7s	*J. R. Ahle*	81
Old Hundredth	L. M.	*G. Franc.*	34
Oliphant	8s, 7s and 4s	*L. Mason*	79
Olivet	6s and 4s	*L. Mason*	151
Olmutz	S. M.	*L. Mason*	134
Olney	S. M.	*L. Mason*	147
Ortonville	C. M.	*T. Hastings*	135
Park Street	L. M.	*F. Venua*	44
Passion Chorale	7s and 6s, D.	*H. L. Hassler*	152
Pleyel's Hymn	7s	*Ig. Pleyel*	59
Portuguese Hymn	11s	*J. Reading*	102, 103
Ratisbon	7s	*J. Neander*	41
Regent Square	8s and 7s, 6l.	*H. Smart*	123
Rest	L. M.	*W. B. Bradbury*	154
Retreat	L. M.	*T. Hastings*	149
Rothwell	L. M.	*Wm. Tansur*	13

St. Agnes	C. M.	J. B. Dykes	15
St. George	C. M.	H. J. Gauntlett	172
St. Hilda	7s and 6s, D.	Knecht & Husband	170
St. Jude	6s, D.	Von Weber	164
St. Peter	C. M.	A. R. Reinagle	93
St. Petersburgh	L. M. 61.	Bortniansky	108
St. Stephen	C. M.	Wm. Jones	3
St. Thomas	S. M.	Wm. Tansur	8
Sabbath	7s, 61.	L. Mason	92
Scotland	12s	John Clarke	136
Seasons	L. M.	Ig. Pleyel	36
Seymour	7s	Von Weber	45
Shepherd	8s, 7s and 4s	W. B. Bradbury	150
Shirland	S. M.	S. Stanley	106
Siloam	C. M.	I. B. Woodbury	118
Silver Street	S. M.	I. Smith	54, 64
Solitude	7s	L. T. Downes	85
State Street	S. M.	J. C. Woodman	121
Stella	L. M.	Jas. Millar	114
Sychar	8s and 7s	J. B. Dykes	144
Tallis' Canon	L. M.	Thos. Tallis	6
Tamworth	8s, 7s and 4s	Ch. Lockhart	56
Telemann's Chant	7s	C. Zeuner	126
Thatcher	S. M.	Handel	11
Toplady	S. M. 61.	T. Hastings	84
Varina	C. M. D.	Rinck-Root	10
Warwick	C. M.	S. Stanley	9
Webb	7s and 6s, D.	G. J. Webb	130
Westminster	C. M.	Jas. Turle	166
Wilmot	8s and 7s	Weber-Mason	120
Windham	L. M.	D. Read	26
Woodworth	L. M.	W. B. Bradbury	156
York	C. M.	Scotch Psalter, 1615	1
Zebulon	H. M.	L. Mason	158
Zion	8s, 7s and 4s	T. Hastings	80

INDEX OF FIRST LINES.

A charge to keep I have	Wesley	58
A few more years shall roll	Bonar	160–161
A mighty fortress is our God	Luther-Hedge	175
Abide with me! fast falls the eventide	Lyte	140
According to Thy gracious word	Montgomery	133
All hail the power of Jesus' name	Perronet	99
All praise to Thee, my God, this night	Ken	6
Am I a soldier of the cross	Watts	33
Angels, from the realms of glory	Montgomery	123
Another six days' work is done	J. Stennett	35
Approach, my soul, the mercy-seat	Newton	89
As pants the hart for cooling streams	Tate & Brady	4
As with gladness men of old	Dix	173
Asleep in Jesus! blessed sleep	Mackay	154
Awake, and sing the song	Hammond	61
Awake, my soul, and with the sun	Ken	5
Awake, my soul, stretch every nerve	Doddridge	65
Awake, our souls; away, our fears	Watts	7
Awake, ye saints, awake	Cotterill	110
Before Jehovah's awful throne	Watts & Wesley	34
Blest be the tie that binds	Fawcett	83
Brief life is here our portion	Bernard-Neale	171
Brightest and best of the sons of the morning	Heber	119
By cool Siloam's shady rill	Heber	118
Children of the heavenly King	Cennick	59
Christ the Lord is risen to-day	Wesley	40
Christ, whose glory fills the skies	Wesley	41
Come, Holy Spirit, come	Hart	70
Come, Holy Spirit, heavenly Dove	Watts	15
Come, let us join our cheerful songs	Watts	9
Come, let us join our friends above	Wesley	57
Come, my soul, thy suit prepare	Newton	90
Come, Thou almighty King	Wesley	55
Come, Thou fount of every blessing	R. Robinson	69

INDEX OF FIRST LINES.

First Line	Author	Page
Come, Thou long-expected Jesus	Wesley	49
Come, we that love the Lord	Watts	8
Day of judgment, day of wonders	Newton	96
Dread Jehovah! God of nations	C. F.	107
Father of heaven, whose love profound	Cooper	111
Father of mercies, in Thy word	Steele	74
Father, whate'er of earthly bliss	Steele	75
Forever with the Lord	Montgomery	134
From all that dwell below the skies	Watts	30
From every stormy wind that blows	Stowell	149
From Greenland's icy mountains	Heber	117
Glorious things of thee are spoken	Newton	95
Glory to Thee, my God, this night	Ken	6
Go to dark Gethsemane	Montgomery	128
God bless our native land	Brooks & Dwight	155
God moves in a mysterious way	Cowper	88
Grace! 'tis a charming sound	Doddridge	64
Great God, what do I see and hear	Collyer & Cotterill	113
Guide me, O Thou great Jehovah	W. Williams	79
Hail! thou once despised Jesus	Bakewell	73
Hail to the Lord's Anointed	Montgomery	130–131
Hark! my soul! it is the Lord	Cowper	85
Hark the glad sound! the Saviour comes	Doddridge	62
Hark! the herald angels sing	Wesley & Madan	39
Hark the song of Jubilee	Montgomery	125
Hark! the voice of love and mercy	Evans	100
Hark what mean those holy voices	Cawood	120
How beauteous are their feet	Watts	11
How firm a foundation, ye saints of the Lord	Keith	103
How oft, alas! this wretched heart	Steele	71
How sweet the name of Jesus sounds	Newton	93
I heard the voice of Jesus say	Bonar	159
I'll praise my Maker with my breath	Watts	32
I love Thy kingdom, Lord	Dwight	106
I would not live alway	Muhlenberg	143
It is not death to die	Malan-Bethune	162
Jerusalem, my happy home	Baker	2
Jerusalem the golden	Bernard-Neale	169
Jesus! and shall it ever be	Grigg & Francis	78
Jesus, hail! enthroned in glory	Bakewell	73
Jesus, I my cross have taken	Lyte	138–139

Jesus, lover of my soul	*Wesley*	43
Jesus, my strength, my hope	*Wesley*	48
Jesus shall reign where'er the sun	*Watts*	31
Jesus, the very thought of Thee	*Bernard-Caswall*	167
Jesus, Thy blood and righteousness	*J. Wesley tr.*	37
Joy to the world! the Lord is come	*Watts*	28
Just as I am, without one plea	*Elliott*	156
Light of those whose dreary dwelling	*Wesley*	51
Lo! He comes with clouds descending	*Cennick*	56
Lord, dismiss us with Thy blessing	*Fawcett*	82
Lord God, the Holy Ghost	*Montgomery*	121
Lord, it belongs not to my care	*Baxter*	1
Lord of the harvest! hear	*Wesley*	47
Lord of the worlds above	*Watts*	29
Love divine, all loves excelling	*Wesley*	53
My faith looks up to Thee	*Palmer*	151
My God, accept my heart this day	*Bridges*	166
My God, how endless is Thy love	*Watts*	16
My God, how wonderful Thou art	*Faber*	163
My soul, be on thy guard	*Heath*	97
Nearer, my God, to Thee	*Adams*	157
O, bless the Lord, my soul	*Watts*	24
O day of rest and gladness	*Wordsworth*	177
O God of Bethel, by whose hand	*Doddridge & Bruce*	63
O happy day, that fixed my choice	*Doddridge*	67
O sacred Head, now wounded	*Gerhardt-Alexander*	153
O Spirit of the living God	*Montgomery*	129
O Thou, from whom all goodness flows	*Haweis*	105
O Thou that hear'st when sinners cry	*Watts*	26
O Thou to Whose all-searching sight	*J. Wesley tr.*	36
O worship the King, all-glorious above	*Grant*	109
Oh could I speak the matchless worth	*Medley*	101
Oh for a closer walk with God	*Cowper*	87
Oh for a heart to praise my God	*Wesley*	46
Oh, where shall rest be found	*Montgomery*	124
O'er the gloomy hills of darkness	*W. Williams*	80
One sole baptismal sign	*G. Robinson*	158
Our God, our help in ages past	*Watts*	27
Our Lord is risen from the dead	*Wesley*	44
Praise to God, immortal praise	*Barbauld*	81
Prayer is the soul's sincere desire	*Montgomery*	122

Rise, my soul! and stretch thy wings?	*Seagrave*	60
Rock of Ages! cleft for me	*Toplady*	84
Safely through another week	*Newton*	92
Salvation! oh the joyful sound	*Watts*	14
Saviour! like a shepherd lead us	*Thrupp*	150
Saviour, Who Thy flock art feeding	*Muhlenberg*	144
Sinners, turn; why will ye die	*Wesley*	45
Softly now the light of day	*Doane*	145
Soldiers of Christ! arise	*Wesley*	54
Songs of praise the angels sang	*Montgomery*	126
Sow in the morn thy seed	*Montgomery*	132
Stand up, my soul! shake off thy fears	*Watts*	13
Sun of my soul, Thou Saviour dear	*Keble*	148
Sweet is the work, my God, my King	*Watts*	25
Sweet the moments, rich in blessing	*Allen & Shirley*	68
The God of Abrah'm praise	*Ollivers*	77
The head that once was crowned with thorns,	*Kelly*	135
The Lord my pasture shall prepare	*Addison*	19
The spacious firmament on high	*Addison*	21
The Spirit in our hearts	*Onderdonk*	147
The voice of free grace cries	*Burdsall*	137
There is a fountain filled with blood	*Cowper*	86
There is a land of pure delight	*Watts*	10
Thou art the Way: to Thee alone	*Doane*	146
Thou, Whose almighty word	*Marriott*	141
Through all the changing scenes of life	*Tate & Brady*	3
Thy way, not mine, O Lord	*Bonar*	165
Watchman, tell us of the night	*Bowring*	142
We give Thee but Thine own	*How*	172
Welcome, sweet day of rest	*Watts*	18
What are these in bright array	*Montgomery*	127
When all Thy mercies, O my God	*Addison*	23
When gathering clouds around I view	*Grant*	108
When I can read my title clear	*Watts*	12
When I survey the wondrous cross	*Watts*	17
When marshall'd on the nightly plain	*White*	114
When streaming from the eastern skies	*Shrubsole*	115
While Thee I seek, protecting Power	*H. M. Williams*	104
While with ceaseless course the sun	*Newton*	91
Ye servants of the Lord	*Doddridge*	66

www.ingramcontent.com/pod-product-compliance
Lightning Source LLC
Chambersburg PA
CBHW020053200426
43197CB00050B/582